The Canadian Alternative

# The Canadian Alternative:
# Cultural Pluralism and Canadian Unity

Edited by Hédi Bouraoui

ECW PRESS
DOWNSVIEW ONTARIO

Canadian Cataloguing in Publication Data

Conference on Cultural Pluralism and the Canadian Unity, York
Universty, 1979.
    The Canadian alternative

Papers presented at the conference held at Stong College, York
University, Oct. 26-27, 1979.

ISBN 0-920802-16-8

1. Multiculturalism - Canada - Congresses.*
I. Bouraoui, Hédi, 1932-    II. Title.

 FC104.C6 1979      305'.0971     C80-094113-6
 F1035.A1C6 1979

*32,922*

Copyright © ECW PRESS, Downsview Ontario 1980

This book has been published with the assistance of the Ontario
Ministry of Culture and Recreation, Multiculturalism Branch.

Printed by Ampersand Printing, Guelph, and typeset by Erin
Graphics, Erin.

The cover was designed by Susan Moshynsky.

Special thanks are due to Olga Cirak and Hélène Issayevitch, who did
the tremendous job of organizing and publicizing the Conference.

Distributed in Canada by
    ECW PRESS
    Stong College, York University
    Downsview Ontario M3J 1P3

# The Canadian Alternative

## Contents

# Introduction

Hédi Bouraoui

The Conference on "Cultural Pluralism and the Canadian Unity," sponsored jointly by Stong College, York University, and the Ontario Advisory Council on Multiculturalism, and held at Stong College on October 26-27, 1979, aimed primarily at opening dialogue between and among the various communities concerned, and between those communities and the university. To that extent it succeeded admirably, though the media and various local interests may have been looking for more pragmatic results and concrete programmes than the Conference was intended to produce.

Remarkably, the various speakers, who had not seen each others' papers in advance, and questions elicited from the floor, all reiterated certain basic themes with which Canadians are intensely preoccupied. If the Conference did not afford any simplistic answers, at the end of two days it at least sharpened the focus of the questions that have been asked, and will continue to be asked, about the role of multiculturalism within the Canadian unity.

Certain patterns began to emerge early. One was the issue of Québec separatism and what relation, if any, it bears to the aspirations of other ethnic communities in Canada. Some speakers, like Alex Chumak, Trustee of the Toronto Board of Education, Ward 1, seemed to feel that only Québec gives other groups special privileges —

through the back door, as it were, by its example — and keeps Canada from becoming a melting pot. "If Québec goes, we all go," said Chumak. Others argued against this notion, pointing out that Québec feels its bilingual-bicultural identity threatened by a policy of "multiculturalism," and is concerned only with its own special status as one of the two original "charter members" of Confederation.

All speakers seemed to agree that the government, both federal and provincial, lacks any clear notion of what a multicultural policy is. Chumak, doing his homework, phoned Queen's Park to ask for a definition of the term, and found that no one could answer. Chumak, Jamshed Mavalwala, Professor of Anthropology at the University of Toronto, Jim Porter of York Univesity, and others all stressed that too often the government associates multiculturalism with exoticism, "the eating and drinking syndrome" manifested in, for instance, Toronto's annual Caravan. They see the government as merely dangling a carrot in front of local community groups, or keeping the lid on. It is much easier to get a local civic celebration funded than a serious study of immigrant groups from the point of view of any scholarly discipline, such as one we know of on the influence of the immigrant imagination on works of Canadian art. But, as Professor Mavalwala sardonically remarked, "No individual lives in Canada *only* to indulge in 'ethnic food' and 'ethnic dance.' " If that is what he wants, he could do it better in his country of origin. In fact, as Porter points out, activities like Caravan are mounted more for the benefit of the outsider, enabling him to practise a form of "soft discrimination" against those whom he perceives as colourful, charming, and essentially vacuous.

It is evident that those who were unable to attend the Conference could have learned a great deal from the enthusiasm, concern, and lively questions. It is to be hoped that in this printed form we will reach a wider, equally responsive audience.

Our approaches were varied and pluridisciplinary: historical, political, sociological, cultural, anthropological — yet all seemed to agree on the major issues:

— to transcend dance and folklore by raising the discussion to an academic level;
— to transcend factionalism — each group seeking its own slice of the pie — in order to promote mutual understanding.

Two thorny questions remain for further discussion and exploration: the role of the native peoples in the Canadian mosaic, and the need to build bridges not only between peoples, or between university and surrounding communities, but also between government and *both* town and gown. Mavalwala and myself struck the keynote at the end by stressing the individual as a whole man with a free will and, at the same time, a product of his total cultural environment, which is more than ethnicity. But how does one work to turn civil servants into social philosophers — or at least into people willing to listen to social philosophy?

York President H. Ian Macdonald, in the opening paper, "New Options for Confederation," addressed himself to the need for constitutional change to accommodate the legitimate aspirations of French Canadians, as well as other regional interests which are feeling increasingly alienated from the Federal system. He pointed out the need to break down the "we"-"they" dichotomy manifested, for example, in the Ontario Government's insensitivity to the desire of Penetang Francophones for a French secondary school. Macdonald was also the first to raise the question of what happens if Québec votes for "sovereignty association."

George Korey, former President of the Ontario Advisory Council on Multiculturalism, felt that "sovereignty association" would effectively take Québec out of Confederation. Jim Porter, on the other hand, took René Lévesque at his word and felt that sovereignty association would *not* result in the breakup of Canada. Macdonald sensibly opined that he hoped someone would clarify the phrasing before Québec votes on the referendum, so at least the Québécois will know exactly what they are voting for. More recent developments in Québec suggest the Québécois are exercising restraint and common sense, and that the tide is shifting back to the Liberals.

Korey, in "Ethnocultural Groups and the Problems of Unity," sees the major defect as insensibility to regional diversity and inflexibility on the federal level. He would like to see a restructured Senate more sensitive to regional differences. Korey feels that we all share the same goal: "to preserve the unity of Canada." Like Wladyslaw Gertler and Rupert Kogler, he values our ties to our varied pasts and feels that if even one generation loses touch with its heritage, it is thereby thrown into the "dust-bin of history."

Kogler's formulation, based on the 1976 census, also raised some questions as to how we define ethnicity in the first place. Several listeners were amused to discover that only the "male side" counts in defining your background, but on the contrary, so does your *mother tongue.*" We are reminded that in the antebellum U.S. South a "Negro" was defined as such by the maternal side only because the paternity could be unknown (often the white plantation-owner). So even our definition of ethnicity is posited on basic assumptions as to who holds the power in society. One group may deprecate assimilation if it leads to collective amnesia, but another, Dr. Mavalwala reminds us, will resist being labelled "ethnic." Clearly the Russian lady proud to answer where she comes from on the basis of her accent is one matter; the black at Dalhousie, whose ancestors have been resident in Canada from the days of the Underground Railway, will, on the other hand, be angry if asked where he comes from on the basis of misconceptions about skin colour.

A Chinese boy in the audience pointed to another example of institutionalized, albeit semi-conscious, racism in the census classification into language groups. It is asserted that one of the largest immigrant increases occurred in the group labelled "Chinese and Japanese": 121%. We all know one of the side-effects of this is complaints about "foreign" students (whether landed immigrants or old Canadians) taking the place of "our kids" (meaning Anglo-Celts) in universities and colleges. As the young man pointed out, such statistics (like those of the Indo-Pakistanis) group people often diametrically opposed in culture, ideology, religion, on the basis of appearance alone (and, further, appearance as perceived by Westerners). Moreover, perhaps the Japanese immigration actually declined; by grouping it with Chinese, no one will ever know.

Stan Kirschbaum points out that, in the words of Erwin Kreutzweiser, "... Canada's unity is in its diversity. ..." Trudeau intended to encourage unity by promoting multiculturalism, but the Québécois came to see it as a threat to their own culture, which "is thereby relegated to a folkloric manifestation." Most Canadians are more contented with multiculturalism on the provincial level than on the federal. This is surely based on geographical reality: there are more Italians than French in Toronto, but at the federal level the British and the French share charter status.

Brodeur's paper takes a somewhat idiosyncratic view of French-Canadian history from a monolithic Roman Catholic perspective unlikely to appeal to the rest of Canada (or indeed to Québécois who separate culture from religion). Johnny Lombardi's paper, based on his "Love" campaign, though non-academic and perhaps naïve in its approach, does, on a grassroots level, address itself to some of the same issues of tolerance and understanding as the scholarly papers of Drs. Mavalwala, Porter, and myself.

Jim Porter's discussion of "Multiculturalism as a Limit of Canadian Life" operates primarily on a theoretical level. He defines the multiculturalist as "one who needs cultural difference to inspire him," seeing nationalism as circular, multiculturalism as elliptical. Many in the audience were left uncertain as to whether Porter was for or against multiculturalism. He admits that clarity is "not the Canadian form," and that decentrism is, but we are never sure whether he regards "dispersion" as a strength or a weakness. Like most of the speakers, he stressed the negativism of Canadian definitions.

If lack of clarity is Canadian, it is also romantic rather than classic, and Porter seems to be applying D. H. Lawrence's "star equilibrium" theory to political science. The analogy between the nation and the couple was already drawn by Denis de Rougemont in his dream of an egalitarian United States of Europe. I questioned from the floor Porter's evident assumption that multiculturalism is irrational.

Chumak's paper, the third in this group, urged us to plant our feet firmly on the ground again and addressed itself to specific issues, such as the reactions of different ethnic groups to the Air Traffic Controller's strike. He urged "the others" in Canada to recognize that they too are deeply implicated in the Québec crisis, and to develop healthy curiosity about others instead of being satisfied with handouts on the local level to put on a multicultural festival. The point from the floor was well taken that both Anglo- and French-Canada need to sensitize themselves to "the others" as well, but Chumak generously was not waiting for others to come forward before he extended his own hand in friendship.

Mrs. Kott's paper called for an expanded dialogue between academe and ethnic communities, indicating that it might well draw on the findings of the rapidly developing science of socio-biology. Through the Bakke case she also raised the issue of minority group rights versus individuals' rights. Many listeners were alarmed at some of the possible ramifications of genetic engineering.

Dr. Mavalwala also dealt with the deeply ingrained prejudice in Canadian life. He stressed that ethnicity is above all a matter of individual choice as to what elements will be incorporated in one's own life. It is important, moreover, that we do not impose our own choice "on the rights of others."

In the final position paper, I tried to pull together several of the threads we had been tracing:

— Canada's tendency to search for definitions as a defense mechanism, usually when the economy is under attack;
— the parallels to ethnic aspirations in the United States;
— transculturalism as a positive alternative to either melting pot or mosaic;
— the need to avoid homogeneity and conformity, the so-called "tyranny of the majority."

Above all, what the Conference achieved was to start us listening to each other. So often multiculturalism is interpreted as a *dialogue de sourds*. But there are patterns, configurations shaping our responses, and to that degree the questions from the floor were at least as illuminating as the papers themselves.[1]

— How does an Oriental react when he finds that all Orientals are grouped together for immigration purposes?
— Is there any such thing as a "black community" in Toronto, when it would have to be composed of peoples from the United States, Canada, Africa, the Caribbean who may have nothing in common but skin colour?
— How do we get civil servants to look at a total, socialized human being, and not at a community representative?
— What price will we pay for Canadian unity?
— What is the relationship between a policy of multiculturalism and one of biculturalism?
— How do nature and nurture interpenetrate?
— Are we so ignorant of the native peoples because, as Porter claims, we are turning away from primitivism? It is surely not culture the Indians and Inuits are lacking, but numbers and political power.

These are just a few of the major issues argued at the Conference. Above all, it forced us to define our own terms — ethnicity, biculturalism, multiculturalism, transculturalism, the "others." The true sources of conflicts of interest are perceived much more clearly when we agree on a common ground of basic definitions. With this initial step forward we can now begin to explore with confidence the numerous contradictions, ambiguities, and unresolved questions that were raised.

If our unity is in our diversity, perhaps the Canadian alternative is a new and unique one in the world, even compared to countries like the United States, most like us, or Belgium or Switzerland. The Conference itself afforded a microcosm of this uniqueness. Unity lies in our diversity only if we listen to each other, and as the Conference progressed over the two days, there was evidently a move away from such opening positions as,

"Where does my community fit into the mosaic?"

to,

"Where do *other* communities fit, and how can I personally relate to them?"

This itself is no mean accomplishment. And obviously the dialogue which has taken place, and which we hope will take place with this book, is the unique Canadian alternative.

### Note

[1]  I am trying to highlight the best of these comments and questions from the floor in this Introduction; they unfortunately proved impossible to record and transcribe verbatim and in their entirety.

HEDI BOURAOUI is presently Master of Stong College, York University, Toronto. He is a Professor of French and Comparative Literature, with a strong interest in Francophone North-African and Caribbean literature. Born in Tunisia, he was raised and educated in France, received his M.A. in English and American literature at Indiana University, and his Ph.D. in Romance Studies at Cornell

University. He has lived and taught for fourteen years in Toronto and has travelled extensively on lecture tours, meeting diverse cultural groups all over the world. He is a poet and a critic, who has published several books of poetry and critical essays. His books *Créaculture I* and *Créaculture II* deal with the interaction of the individual and his milieu in the comparative framework of Europe and North America. He is pursuing his interest in Cultural Studies in a Multicultural Context through the academic programmes of Stong College.

## Note

The immigration focus more than anything else has characterized the historical development of our nation. Over time, it has dramatically changed the demographic nature of our society and still continues to do so. If we value our democratic freedoms, rights and privileges, it is imperative that as a nation we recognize and respect the cultural diversity in our midst.

It is my strong conviction that far from being a somewhat unfortunate legacy of immigration, our cultural pluralism is at the very heart and core of our uniqueness, of our identity as a nation. It is for this reason that I wholeheartedly welcome this collection of papers written by community leaders and academics on the subject of "Cultural Pluralism and the Canadian Unity". I sincerely hope that it may inspire others in further exploring the essence of this country which I am proud to have served and represented as Minister of State for Multiculturalism.

Steve E. Paproski
January 1980

# Towards New Options for Confederation

## H. Ian Macdonald

Some of you here may well have been present at York University just over two years ago for the *Destiny Canada Destinée* Conference. Our purpose then was to get to know one another better, to understand our hopes and our apprehensions, our likes and our dislikes, our biases and our preferences. That phase in the recent Confederation debates was exceedingly important. It is a phase which continues through the countless unity groups right across the country, and within the debate and introspection which has become part of our national fabric.

However, there is a time to debate and a time to believe, a time to talk and a time to act, a time to dream and a time to decide. I believe that such a time is now upon us. We must put aside the easy generalizations such as "the need for constitutional reform," "more decentralization," "the redesign of Confederation" and consider hard specifics. Happily, a number of those specifics have now been placed on the table for our consideration and future direction, including those incorporated in the two Reports of the Ontario Advisory Committee on Confederation, the First in April, 1978, and the Second in March, 1979. I trust that they will contribute along with other such documents to the re-confederation of Canada. Yet, all the reports in the world will not help us to preserve Canada, to adapt Confederation and to ensure a happy future in this country, unless we can demonstrate a different attitude of mind towards the current realities of Canadian life and the composition of the Canadian mosaic.

This is a Conference on Cultural Pluralism and Canadian Unity. Consequently, I am well aware that your concern during the next two days will be with the multicultural reality of Canada and the choices which we face in a society of such composition. Others more competent than I will be dealing with the technical characteristics of that situation. What I wish to deal with today, however, is the ancient but enduring problem of English-French relations in Canada. I am well aware that, among a large number of Canadians of neither Anglo-Saxon nor French ancestry, there is often a resentment that the bilateral debate appears to ignore the rest of our citizenry. However, we cannot deny our history and the reality of all that has composed it. My fundamental proposition is simply that, if we cannot display the attitude of mind necessary to resolving questions of the English-French relationship, then we will all be the poorer for it and our chances of achieving the resolution of our broader problems will be diminished. Those who have come from backgrounds other than English-speaking or French-speaking should not feel that the apparent Canadian pre-occupation with English-French relations suggests an indifference to our multicultural reality.

What then is the status of national unity today? Confederation was an act of man and an article of faith. It was a response to historical, geographical, and political circumstances in which we agreed to embark upon building a nation on the northern half of this continent based on two principal languages and a variety of regions. In the intervening years, much has changed in the workings of Canadian Confederation. The two corner-stones of any federal system are its constitutional underpinnings and its fiscal arrangements. In both cases, we have seen important changes through the medium of inter-governmental agreement as well as judicial interpretation of the constitution. In any such changes, there is a process of steady adaptation to the consensus of the time; it becomes an act of political will to carry out those changes.

I have always believed that the Canadian federation was a magnificent achievement and that, if circumstances had not dictated the formation of a federal system in Canada, then we would have done well to invent one. Such are the regional characteristics of Canada that a decentralized form of government is essential. The BNA Act has served us well in Canada which is, after all, one of the longest surviving and most successful federations in the world. Both in terms of our optimism for the future and our commitment to our country, we should never forget that fact. Equally, we must be forever prepared to develop and to adapt Confederation to the requirements of the day. In my opinion, we have reached that stage where some major redesign of the Canadian Confederation is essential if we are to survive. It is unfortunate that we did not attend to this matter ten years ago or even sooner. The need has not sprung upon us overnight, but has been the result of gathering forces over a period of time.

The most pressing requirement today is to fortify the leadership of the moderates. I believe that the vast majority of Canadians want to maintain a united Canada and are willing to make the sacrifices necessary to achieve that objective. However, too often the strongest voices would appear to be those of the intractable or the extremists. What I have always believed is that we require the moderates to be encouraged in every quarter of our country and then for those who understand the intricacies of federalism to put forward options that those moderate forces can consider and in which they can find some hope for the resolution of our past difficulties. In such a process, risks must be faced, particularly in the political system.

Since the Quebec election of November 15, 1976, Canada has been caught up in a debate of fundamental principles unprecedented since the negotiations leading to Confederation in 1867. All of this points to one central reality: basic changes are necessary to re-establish the Canadian Confederation on a more secure foundation to meet the challenges of the future.

At the same time, this very fact of intense introspection and national self-searching — in the rest of Canada as well as in Quebec — shows that the will to go on still exists. There is a Canadian ideal and we are all Canadians, if only we can define ourselves and shape our institutions to meet our needs for nationhood. This is not only a matter of accommodating Quebec, but also of satisfying the new and old grievances of the West, the Atlantic provinces, and the North.

Even in Ontario, sometimes regarded elsewhere as the major beneficiary of Confederation, there is at present a feeling of alienation from our federal institutions. Moreover, there have been too many federal-provincial conferences in which ministers from the two levels of government appeared as adversaries in confrontation rather than

17

joint architects of national policy.

A few months ago, I was sitting on a park bench on the Plains of Abraham in Quebec City trying to see our nation in perspective. I had been pondering a remark made to me by some students just a year ago at this time. I had pointed out to them a notice that had been placed in the *In Memorium* column of *The Globe and Mail* in respect to the memory of General Wolfe who died that day in the year 1759. These two young people said to me: "What possible significance can a battle fought between two imperial powers over two hundred years ago have for us?" The answer, unfortunately, is that it has much significance because it has set the tone for the two hundred years of intervening history. Today we are witnessing the high point of that historic evolution.

I had a variety of thoughts that morning on the Plains of Abraham. In the first place, I realized once again that the historic inheritance of the intervening two hundred years belongs to me as it belongs to all Canadians, and that it is one of the great strengths of this nation — not a weakness. I do not want to see that destroyed or simply wither away. Secondly, I thought of what Canada had always meant to so many people, people such as my own mother and father who left school in Scotland at age fourteen and came to this country, independently and on their own at age sixteen, in the belief that a true sense of personal freedom was available here. Thirdly, I thought of the way in which Canadians had always worked at providing the accommodation necessary to keep this country together, and to render it unique in the sense that our federation is one of the longest surviving federations in the world. Finally, I thought of the manner in which we have created institutions and considered them as flexible and adaptable rather than as fixed for all time.

Today, however, I am concerned that we may have lost much of those basic ingredients in Canadian life. There is a danger that meanness and self-interest can frustrate the manifest destiny of this nation; I for one am not prepared to see that happen, nor should you be. But I strongly believe that the future of Canada will be determined largely by our attitude of mind, and our attitude of mind must be progressive, compassionate, innovative, and creative. Is it?

During a discussion of Confederation at Queen's University, Principal Watts made the following comment: "Certainly it is quite clear in the history of many other federations that the most critical period arises when there is common agreement that the current constitution will not do, and yet there is no agreement about what will replace it. I think this is the dangerous situation we find ourselves in as a country now." I find a fairly wide measure of agreement among people that we should be moving to adapt Canada and its institutions to a new federalism, that will keep Canada together and strengthen the nation. This requires a great deal of mature and dispassionate consideration. And yet, whenever suggestions are made for change, the gates of hell open up to devour those who dared to make them. I hope that all of us will take seriously the various proposals that are now being put forward. It is disconcerting to our Ontario Advisory Committee on Confederation, as I know it must be to other groups, to find those who immediately reject suggestions out of hand either because they have not made the effort to understand them or more often because they affect their own narrow vested interests. Do we want Canada to survive or don't we? Do we want to place the interest of this country ahead of our parochial concerns? Do we want Canada to exist in an atmosphere of pettiness and meanness or do we want to strive to achieve fulfillment of our great promise through the route of magnanimity, open-mindedness, and forbearance? I hope this will be the attitude which we will all take to the serious proposals of various bodies as I trust others will take to the proposals of the Advisory Committee on Confederation, and, indeed, as I hope the Ontario Government itself will take to the advice that we have rendered.

I recall so well at the *Confederation of Tomorrow* Conference when the then Premier Ike Smith of Nova Scotia said: "What is more important, Canada or the constitution? If the country is in trouble by all means let us change the constitution." As I suggest, the most important question is the matter of attitude of mind and behaviour. How easy it is for that attitude to degenerate. Nothing is more important than the attitude of mind that is expressed toward our French-speaking fellow citizens because it reflects the feeling of Canadians to one another. I am convinced that French Canadians will want to remain in Canada in direct proportion to the belief that they are welcome here.

Recently, I sat beside an old gentleman at a softball game in a small town in Ontario and, in talking about these questions, he said to me: "Well, I don't know much about Quebec, but I sure love Canada." That comment, made in all innocence, speaks volumes. Many of us simply do not know enough about other parts of the country, particularly Quebec, or else we have strong views based on our sense of history or our personal attitude which may or may not be in the best interests of the country. The gentleman I described said he did not know much about Quebec, but he loved Canada. The question is: does he love it enough to accept the changes which, in my opinion, are necessary and inevitable where Quebec and French Canada are concerned? Too many of us have tended to think of the so-called "Quebec problem" and discuss it in terms of "we" and "they." How can we talk about "we" and "they" when we are talking about twenty-three percent of the population of Canada where Quebec francophones are concerned or twenty-seven percent of Canada where French Canadians are concerned? This, in other words, is a major part of our country and, if we love our country and want it to stay together, we must be prepared to do what is necessary to achieve that goal.

Why do so many of us persist in regarding the two languages of this country as a liability rather than as an asset? To confer on others their rightful language rights does not diminish the rest of us in any way; to be a nation of two official languages is surely an asset and not a liability; to have a special history combining a native population, two principal languages, and many cultures should provide a source of strength and distinction as we seek to co-exist with a powerful and culturally aggressive neighbour.

Unfortunately, the whole language question has been vested with a number of myths, in part to do with policies of bilingualism, and many misunderstandings. There is an immense difference between "shoving French down the throats of English-speaking Canadians" and granting language rights to the French-speaking minority. In the correspondence one reads in the newspapers, the following arguments are raised:

1. "The French-Canadians should have no language rights." In answer to that, surely twenty-seven percent of the population and the members of one of the two founding peoples are entitled to such rights.

2. "Encouraging the French language poses a threat to those of us who are English-speaking." Can anyone seriously believe such a suggestion in a continent of 240 million people of whom more than 230 million speak English, and in a world in which the language of commerce is and likely will remain English?

3. "French-language services will be an unnecessary public expenditure." Of course they cost money, but what price are we prepared to pay in the interest of national unity? Alternatively, what would the cost be of Canada breaking up?

4. "We will all be obliged to learn French." No one has suggested, least of all the Francophones of Canada, that English-speaking Canadians must learn French. That is not to say, however, that we should disregard the added dimension which a capacity in our second language would bring to the lives of English-speaking Canadians.

We all bear part of the responsibility for the outcome of these matters. It is a responsibility not for government alone but one for all people to share. I hope that those who play a role, as you do, in the human affairs of this nation will take every opportunity to assume that additional responsibility.

Meanwhile, we require certain qualities as never before in the history of our Confederation, particularly, patience and forbearance. At the same time, certain actions can assume a high degree of symbolism which may well determine the final outcome of the issue. Let me illustrate by three examples.

Painful as it may be, and I realize it is difficult for someone outside the Province of Quebec to make such a declaration, I believe we must be patient in the short run about the direction of language legislation in Quebec. Surely in the long run the commercial reality of Quebec's position within the North American context, and indeed, the reality that English is the language of commerce, will ensure that English as a second language is widespread in Quebec, and that the final result will be a population in that province equally at home in either language. However, as the Government of Quebec attempts to assert the supremacy of the French language by appearing to make it exclusive, can we withstand the stress until the necessary balance is asserted?

In the same way, those who face decisions such as the Directors of the Sun Life Assurance Company of Canada must be prepared to take a longe-range view and to recognize that a decision to make a commitment to Quebec is also a decision for a commitment to Canada, and that a decision to abandon it can make separation a self-fulfilling prophecy.

However, the third example is much closer to home, and I refer to the difficult question of a French-language secondary school in

21

Penetanguishene. I am well aware of all the practical and economic arguments against the building of that school. I am conscious of the extreme opinions as well as the more moderate attitudes. However, I earnestly hope that it will be possible for the Government of Ontario to arrive at a solution which both recognizes French-language rights in that part of the province, and makes adequate provision for the entitlement of our Franco-Ontarian citizens there. That situation has two important characteristics. In the first place, it tests the people of this province in terms of the generosity of heart and spirit in recognizing our Franco-Ontarian citizens. In the second place, it telegraphs to the citizens of Quebec, at a time when they are deciding whether they have a place in Canada, something of the basic attitudes of the people of this province. Whereas it is true there are constitutional differences between the language situation in Ontario and Quebec, as demonstrated by Article 133 of the British North America Act, it is equally true that the attitude of the French-speaking citizen in Quebec toward his English-speaking brother in that province has a parallel in the reverse situation in Ontario. If, by our behaviour, we cannot say to the people of Quebec that we want to preserve French-language rights in Ontario, then it is difficult for me to believe that the French-speaking citizens of Quebec will consider that the rest of Canada truly wants to preserve a place for them.

What we must do, above all, is to maintain a true dialogue based on two ultimate objectives:

1. a commitment to build Canada into a more effective united nation;

2. a willingness to share in Quebec's struggle to assert its sense of nationhood within the Canadian Confederation. When the people of Quebec take the final decision about their ultimate future, I, for one, want to feel that every effort has been made to lead us towards new options for Confederation — options that will guarantee the future unity, vitality, and maturity of our country.

Finally, let me stress once again that I understand the special feeling of the ethnic communities in Canada that they have been left out of the dialogue. Quite properly, they remind the rest of us that the future of Canada will not be based only on the resolution of the French-English issue, but on the resolution of the Canadian issue. However, all of Canada will also benefit from a happy resolution of English-French relations, particularly from a rejection of separatism in the forthcoming referendum in Quebec.

Thus, I would ask you to consider one exceedingly important and relevant situation soon to be faced by Canadians. At some point over the next few months, I believe the Parti Québécois could still win the referendum simply because it will be phrased in a manner to appeal to a majority. At that point, we face the real test. The PQ must explain the details of sovereignty-association, and the Quebec Liberal Party its proposals for the re-design of Confederation. Unless we wish to give the people no alternative to separation, we must be prepared to accept basic changes in Confederation.

At this critical point, the fact of leadership in the federal government becomes critical. The federal government must be able and willing to negotiate constitutional change acceptable to Quebec without, at the same time, alienating the rest of Canada. I believe that the federal government can and must meet that objective.

Meanwhile, I believe we have every reason to be optimistic about the future of Canada. The story is told about the enthusiastic golfer who began to contemplate whether there would be golf in the hereafter. He became so preoccupied with this question that he consulted his priest one evening and the priest agreed to try and find the answer for him that night. The following morning the priest met with the golfer again and said he had communicated with God and he had the answer. However, he said: "I have good news and bad news. The good news is that yes, indeed, there is a golf course in heaven. The bad news is that your tee-off time is ten o'clock tomorrow morning."

I do hope that these remarks will have helped to outline the course ahead, to reveal some of the traps, but to suggest that the fairway is open to us if we wish to move forward.


H. IAN MACDONALD, O.C., B.COM., M.A., B.Phil., LL.D., became President of York University in July 1974, after serving in the Provincial Government as Deputy Treasurer and Deputy Minister of Economics and Intergovernmental Affairs. He holds memberships in a large number of national and international associations, and is a Director of Canadian General Electric Company Ltd., Rockwell International of Canada Ltd., The Canadian Opera Company, a member of the Economic Council of Canada, and Chairman of the Ontario Advisory Committee on Confederation.

# Ethnocultural Groups and the Problems of Unity

George Korey

Addressing a conference on Cultural Pluralism and Canadian Unity, one is deeply conscious of the fact that there are here representatives of many ethnocultural groups, different from one another in country of origin, in mother tongue, in religion, in the colour of our skins — and yet we all know that we are in many ways similar, and that we share a common goal, and a common purpose.

We have the same hopes for a secure and peaceful life; we have the same ambition for ourselves and our children; we share the same fears and anxieties; but above all we share the same great desire to preserve the unity of Canada.

I believe we may agree that those things which divide us can be reconciled and harmonized with those things which unite us, that those qualities within us which make us different, need not separate us. It is in this spirit that I want to share with you a few thoughts at this conference.

Nearly one-third of the population of Canada are either immigrants themselves or children of immigrants. Some of them have come to this country to escape the tensions, the animosities, the repressions and persecutions of their former homelands, others have come because they know Canada is a country rich in human resources, a country in which they and their children might live better, more pleasant lives.

I believe very strongly that cultural diversity enriches all Canadians with a great variety of human experience and that the concept of multiculturalism encourages every individual and ethnic group to retain their traditions, cultural values, and identity, whilst simultaneously enriching the fabric of the national Canadian culture with their own particular contributions.

Countless ages of ancestors have bequeathed to us a treasure-house of cultural and religious values. If but a single generation loses its love for the past, this accumulation of ethnocultural riches may easily and swiftly be discarded in the dust-bin of history. It is our responsibility to preserve these values, to develop them, and to pass them on to those who will come after us.

The fact that immigrants preserve their own heritage and retain the basic sense of belonging to their own ethnic groups in total promotes rather than detracts from the wider loyalty to the community and to the country of their adoption.

The very essence of multiculturalism permits the ethnic groups to preserve the feeling that they are connected directly with the tradition and the human experience of those parts of the world from which they came. They should continue to maintain and develop their cultural values within the Canadian context because to be a good Canadian does not imply a denial of one's heritage — in fact, the reverse is true.

Personally, I can see Canada as a cultural commonwealth where all groups can contribute to its growth and where each individual shares Canadian pride in national achievement. The Federal and Provincial Governments' commitment to multiculturalism is very gratifying and, I am certain, particularly welcomed by the ethnic groups. It is based on the understanding that multiculturalism and multicultural interaction and co-operation penetrating cultural barriers is a road leading to a smoother integration rather than to isolation and fragmentation. And yet while we share generously in the cultural bounty which now is as much a part of our environment as are our natural resources, we are concerned, deeply concerned, about the future of this great country.

There is a growing awareness among us, who have learned to love and respect this nation, that the next few years will determine whether Canada will survive as a united country. In November 1976 this danger was presented to us by the election of the Parti Québécois. In the intervening three years, as the peril of separation seemed to become less urgent, the nation has yielded to apathy, a feeling that somehow circumstances will right themselves and that Canada will remain united.

Canada faces many problems, of both political and economic nature, in this eighth decade of the twentieth century. But none surely is more important than the need to find a formula which will weld Canada together as a single nation, one and indivisible.

As a former Chairman of the Ontario Advisory Council on Multiculturalism and member of the Advisory Committee on Confederation, I have become profoundly conscious of the difficulties which must be resolved. And it is in the best self-interest of all the ethnocultural groups that these difficulties by resolved because unity of Canada is not only a matter of discussion between French- and English-speaking Canadians, but it is vital to all those who came here and have chosen this country as their own. The spirit of integration of different heritages and traditions has led to the generally accepted concept of Canadianism, diverse in its cultural background, but united in its common goals, aspirations, and love of this country. And to us — ethnocultural groups of Canada — the Confederation of 1867 and the spirit of Charlottetown are closer than the day of the battle on the Plains of Abraham. In our opinion those of our compatriots who derive English supremacy from one victorious battle are just as wrong as those who derive all their grievances from one battle lost two hundred years ago. The Canada of today is a result of a great vision realized with conscious effort to build a great country and a nation.

But what is appalling to us and what scares us is that one of the great problems facing Canada today is an unbelievable ignorance of English Canada about French Canada and the same is true about ignorance of French Canada about English Canada. This is quite clear for somebody like myself who for twenty years has lived in Québec and can safely claim to understand both parts. Therefore, in my eyes, the fact that on the Federal Task Force of National Unity there was no representation of people from other than English and French ethno-cultural groups, was quite frankly a very serious mistake.

It is now almost three years since the election of Premier Lévesque and the separatist government in Québec and during the time since the Parti Québécois took power certain things have become clear.

*No one can be under any illusion* about the goals of the present government of Québec. It is dedicated to taking Québec out of Confederation and establishing an independent sovereign country. It would prefer some type of economic association with the rest of Canada, but that is secondary to the main goal of achieving political independence.

There is also a growing consensus throughout Canada that the present federal government structure must be modified and changed to meet the needs of a changing country. This means different division of powers between federal and provincial governments.

Many people who observe the present situation are convinced that the most immediate need in keeping the nation together is not only to defeat the referendum proposed by the Premier of Québec but to defeat the PQ at the next election in Québec. Until a party dedicated to keeping Québec within Confederation is elected within Québec many feel that the separation issue — *regardless of the outcome of referendums — will not be settled.* But even if Premier Lévesque can be defeated *at an election, serious modifications* in the *constitution will be necessary.*

As a result of my work on the Advisory Committee on Confederation, I have become profoundly conscious of the difficulties which must be resolved. I know how deeply the French Canadians value their spiritual, cultural, and religious identity, the sacrifices they have made to preserve them, and their determination to endure as a distinct entity. But I have also been witness to the passionate devotion of countless men and women to the concept of a united Canadian nation. They understand that there must be changes, psychological no less than constitutional. The vast majority of them are happy to accept these changes and are willing to make the essential adjustments and the necessary compromises.

In this spirit of goodwill rests the hope that Canada may prove that cultural diversity is consistent with national unity and that difference may provide an opportunity for spiritual growth and cultural enrichment.

In this arduous process of preserving Canadian unity, the ethno-cultural minorities have a critical role to play. They constitute one-third of the population of Canada. They are men and women of courage, ambition, and intelligence, eager to build their lives anew in what they see as a great and promising land. They or their parents left their homelands because they saw Canada as a land of economic opportunity. Also, they felt that in Canada they would be free to exercise those democratic rights which are man's rightful inheritance, because they would be free of the hatreds and antagonisms of the Old World, and because they knew that they would not be required to surrender their ethnic individuality. They acknowledge their debt to the dedication and devotion of the French Canadians to their own ethnocultural and religious values. They understand that as they fight for the rights of the French Canadians as one of the two "founding peoples" who gave this nation birth, so they fight for their own languages, their own cultures, their own religions.

As a result of my work on the Advisory Committee on Confederation I think I can safely say that a combination of insensitivity to regional diversity and imbalance of political power is the basic flaw in our current federal system.

Therefore, there must be a major restructuring of existing federal-provincial institutions and the development of some new ones in order to accommodate regional needs.

Presently, the Senate does not represent provincial interests as it should. Therefore, it should probably be restructured to be able to better represent the interests of the provinces.

A lot of tension in federal-provincial relations would be alleviated and the duplication of legislative effort of both levels of government could be eliminated if federal legislation had to be passed by an Upper House comprised of the various regional interests.

Such a restructured Upper House could have a veto on some matters, including amendments to the constitution and laws that require a national consensus or laws that directly affect the provinces.

There are also several highly important federal boards and regulatory commissions that set federal policy on a wide range of national matters. These include the Bank of Canada, the Canadian Transport Commission, the CRTC, and the Canadian Development Corporation. The decisions which these federal bodies make have a profound effect on the development of the country as a whole and upon provincial priorities, and yet presently the provinces have no voice in the appointment of the directors of these bodies which formulate such important policies for the whole country.

The new constitution of Canada should allow the provinces to have influence on these federal boards and commissions so that they can function as truly multi-governmental bodies.

We also have to reassess the basic principles of the division of powers between the two levels of government — federal and provincial. Maybe rather than unilaterally defining the national interest, the federal cabinet should have a more coordinating role with provincial governments — which are often able to provide regionally sensitive and more accountable ways of governing to the citizens.

For the ethnocultural groups it is of paramount importance to have in a new constitution the assurance of basic freedoms, basic political and human rights.

Finally, we need a constitution with more flexibility to accommodate the aspirations of different regions of the country. For one of the provinces, preserving a culture and language is of paramount concern; to other provinces, unequal economic opportunity is the greatest problem requiring solution; to still other regions, developing a sound and lasting industrial base is of greatest importance. What we need is a constitution and a division of powers which can accommodate these legitimate aspirations.

We believe that the ethnocultural minorities, because of their historic experience, have a unique understanding of the problems Canadians generally are facing. While they do not minimize the importance of economic and constitutional factors in the pursuit of national unity, they believe that even more critical is a knowledge of the nature of nationalist movements. These movements are based on considerations which are not linked to economics and constitutions, but are rather founded on group loyalties, group pride, and group aspirations.

This struggle for Canadian unity in view of the expected forthcoming constitutional changes is not one from which the ethnocultural communities can withdraw. This is a challenge which the ethnocultural groups must accept.

We Canadians have, during the past quarter-century, accomplished a great deal in our effort to make Canada a good country in which to work and live. The spirit of cultural pluralism or multiculturalism has captured the imagination of the Canadian people. Diversity has become acceptable. Difference has become a virtue. Racial, religious, and linguistic attributes have been recognized as factors which enrich all Canadians. There has been an almost universal willingness, even a desire, to share in the tremendous gifts which are being brought to Canada by hundreds of thousands of recent arrivals, all of them with their own contributions to make to the society which welcomed them.

But Canada is facing a very difficult epoch in her history. She faces urgent economic problems, whose impact will probably become more oppressive before the problems are solved. She faces the danger of a disruption of the unity which was the great glory of a nation extending, unbroken, from the mist-shrouded harbour of Prince Rupert to the Grand Banks off the coast of Newfoundland.

If unemployment increases, if inflation reduces the standard of living of Canadians and creates uneasiness among those who have set aside some meagre savings to protect themselves against the vicissitudes of illness and age, we may expect that tensions will increase, that tempers will rise, that mutual understanding will become more difficult to achieve. Tolerance is often a product of prosperity. If the Canadian economy weakens further, competition for jobs and wages will become keener. The generous spirit which has animated Canadians during the past few decades of uninterrupted progress may tend to weaken, permitting the introduction of an atmosphere of suspicion and mistrust which will leave none of us untouched. There may well be a tendency for individuals to withdraw inwards, to see their personal problems as their paramount concern. They may be tempted to turn away from those who differ from them, to reject those who have newly come to Canada, to see them not as partners in a common enterprise but as competitors in a fierce and unrelenting struggle for survival.

It is not too soon for Canada's ethnocultural communities, which means *all* of us who share a common destiny, to consider their responsibilities in the light of those problems and the new realities. Now, more than ever before, the institutions which have been built up to protect minorities must be strengthened and extended. Greater emphasis must be placed on the Human Rights Commission, more effort must be expended to ensure that Fair Accommodation and Fair Employment Practice Acts are strong enough to perform their functions, swiftly and successfully.

But much more must be done. The law is only one aspect of the continuing fight for equality for all Canadians — citizens and immigrants alike: It can resolve only partially the problems which ethnocultural communities face. There must be a concerted effort among all of us to reduce racial tension, to share our values with each other, to struggle against any wave of reaction which may impede the progress which has been made in the effort to humanize our society and to make us responsible for each other's welfare in an often harsh and difficult world.

We must continue to pursue those ideals which have inspired us for many years. We must ensure equality for all Canadians regardless of race, religion, and ethnic origin. But we must also come together more frequently, and more intimately, as Canadians. We have a responsibility to our own ethnic groups, and we have also an overriding responsibility to ensure that Canada shall be, what we, or our immigrant parents, dreamt it would be — a great united country, a land of equality and opportunity. This could be done only if all of us join forces in the critically important tasks facing this nation.

We all believe in the ideal of a Canada in which a wide variety of spiritual, cultural, religious, and linguistic communities share common goals, common hopes, common visions of a brighter and happier future for themselves and for the united country. Let's commit ourselves anew to the effort to make an appreciable, if modest, contribution to this end. It may be that Canadian ethnocultural groups will provide this very necessary ingredient which will cement the unity of this great country.


GEORGE KOREY is former chairman of the Ontario Advisory Council on Multiculturalism and also a member of the Ontario Advisory Committee on Confederation. Dr. Korey, born in Poland, held positions in the Polish Foreign Service, and took part in negotiations in treaties and international agreements. Graduated from Cracow, Poland, with a Master of Laws degree, he pursued post-graduate studies at the Academy of Political and Social Sciences in Warsaw, the University of Bucharest in Rumania, the Institute of International Law, the University of Frieburg, West Germany, and the University of Tubingen, West Germany.

# Cultural Diversity and Canadian Unity:
# The Political Imperative

Stanislav J. Kirschbaum

The juxtaposition of cultural diversity and Canadian unity may seem to some like a juxtaposition of irreconcilable concepts, both theoretically and empirically. Cultural diversity conjures up images of international rather than intra-national activity, and Canadian unity suggests the presence of a unifying force that tends more toward uniformity than diversity. The scholarly literature that deals in one form or another with either or both of these concepts seems to suggest that they are indeed mutually exclusive. Paradoxically, most scholars are quick to condemn the historical and logical outcome of this irreconcilability without really examining the alternatives. Nor do they put into question the premises of their argument. Our purpose is not only to look at the arguments presented in the literature, but to point out as well that there is a political imperative in juxtaposing cultural diversity and Canadian unity that transcends our own national context.

That Canadian, or more broadly speaking, national unity has become a question of paramount importance in the modern era is the result of an historical development which has yet to complete itself. We are referring here to the appearance and growth of the ideology of nationalism and of nationalist movements.

An examination of the history of nationalism must lead one,

however, to acknowledge the diversity of its manifestations in time and space. The main scholars on nationalism — Hans Kohn, Carlton Hayes, Boyd Shafer, among others — have shown how nationalism arose in opposition to the feudal order in Europe. Elie Kédourie traced its intellectual antecedents and development to show how society had moved from the universalism of Christianity and the Holy Roman Empire to the fragmentation of Christendom into states and faiths. Nationalism was the response not only to new intellectual approaches, but also to expanded economic and social activity. This new anthropocentrism necessitated new forms of social organization. As Boyd Shafer wrote:

> During the nineteenth century, particularly in Western Europe and the United States, liberalism and nationalism grew together, liberalism especially in its democratic aspects, contributed to the growth of nationalism. For it was within and through the nation-state, not a church or an international organization, that the individual obtained his freedom and the vote. In obtaining these, he felt he belonged; when he became a citizen he became, in fact, part of the nation, part of its government.[1]

The fact that nationalism also came to serve conservative and authoritarian regimes need not concern us here. What one must stress, however, is the fact that nationalist ideology and nationalist movements did develop within the confines of states whose social and cultural composition was rarely homogeneous. In the context of the time and the struggle against feudalism, the early nationalists fought primarily for the answer to the question of who controls the state: the monarch or the people. Once the answer became clear in the century that followed the French and American revolutions, the state then became the mediator for individual as well as collective needs. Louis XIV's statement "L'Etat, c'est moi" became "L'Etat, c'est nous." And as the functions of the state increased in scope and variety, there grew the belief, as Carlton Hayes writes, that "the state, particularly the national state, can and should promote human progress."[2]

The struggle against feudalism was successful in those states which had embarked on the path of economic and social growth. This growth brought a further development in nationalist ideology whose relevance is still very much with us today. As Shafer writes: "The cultural needs and economic and social problems became so vast and complex that only an institution to which men are loyal and which possessed great power could meet them. This institution, in the fullest sense, became the nation-state."[3]

It is interesting to note that the literature on nationalism has concentrated primarily on the definitions, meanings, and consequences of the fusion of the state with the nation. Despite the difficulties in finding an acceptable definition of the nation, scholars, along with nationalists, have persisted in seeing the state-nation fusion as logical and inevitable. That nationalists should do so is understandable. The focus of their activity is the collectivity with which they identify, which they define and whose destiny they seek to control. By taking over the state from the monarchy and the aristocracy, nationalists brought the state closer to the people by offering jobs, by basically taking care of all citizens. As Shafer points out, the national governments "in these ways turned the eyes of more and more of their citizens toward the nation. At the same time forces encroaching upon the nation-state from without had a similar effect."[4] State sovereignty became national sovereignty and as René Lévesque has pointed out: "Sovereignty, quite simply and naturally, for us as for other peoples, is the fact of acceding to full national responsibility."[5]

It is sufficient to point out the further directions in which nationalism has travelled and might yet go to perceive some of the difficulties in this line of thought. Some scholars have seen fascism as the ultimate consequence[6] of nationalist policies while others have reserved judgement on this proposition without necessarily excluding it.[7] Some, in an effort to deal with the negative aspects of nationalism, have returned to the notion of universalism, to the consideration of the development of a world government[8] or else have suggested that nationalism "like other faiths in the past, could not completely captivate and subjugate men, and might possibly be submerged or disappear as other environmental conditions arise in the future."[9]

However pertinent or laudable these considerations might be, they do not help us to appreciate and cope with the present situation, especially in Canada. Empirically, emphasis on the preeminence of the nation leads to the further re-drawing of the map, the break-up of the majority of the countries existing today as each national community demands its own state. This is the logic of national self-determination. It is perhaps then not so ironical that the statesmen preaching self-determination have also refused to see it through. The Versailles settlement is a case in point. Not only did the break-up of Austria-Hungary result in the creation of two small multinational states, Czecho-Slovakia and Yugoslavia, but as Hayes has pointed out: "The gentlemen who dictated the Peace of Paris in 1919-1920 honestly tried to recognize and validate the principle of nationality, but they represented, of course, the victors in the Great War and they were naturally disposed both to reward their own national states and to punish the vanquished."[10] It is not necessary to elaborate upon the point that the Versailles settlement led to the outbreak of World War II. Just as it is impossible to put into effect the principle of self-determination, it is likewise fruitless to hope for the appearance of a world government. The activities of the United Nations Organization since its creation make this perfectly clear.

The road out of this impasse lies in the re-examination of the premises on which the ideology of nationalism has developed. Our enquiry will be made along two lines: one is the meaning and importance of the concept of nation, the other is the role of the state.

In his seminal work, *The Idea of Nationalism*, Hans Kohn wrote: "Nationality is a historical and political concept, and the words 'nation' and 'nationality' have undergone many changes in meaning. It is only in recent history that man has begun to regard nationality as the center of his political and cultural activity and life."[11] He goes on to point out that this concept has always existed as a state of mind, an idea which goes back to ancient Hebrews and Greeks but which remained basically latent until it was given a political form in the modern era, the modern state. In effect, what has always existed is a living and active corporate will within self-defined communities to live and do things together. Either language, race, geography, religion, or a shared past, factors which are often used to define a nation, but none of which is necessary for the definition, has been used to delineate further the boundaries of the collective will in time and space. The interaction between communities has determined the survival of any one community and some communities have disappeared while others have grown to become major actors within a given geographical area. Communities have also coexisted side by side; Europe's multinational empires before the advent of nationalism were an amalgam of races, cultures, languages, and faiths.

The fact that we speak of nations today does not automatically exclude other forms of collective organization. At one end of the scale, there exist communities which social scientists define as tribes, clans, ethnic, and cultural groups. At the other, since 1957, the classical nations of Western Europe have been on the path of economic, social, and political integration, creating in effect a new sort of multinational state. Despite such examples, the nation is the one definition of the community to which an individual most often gives his loyalty. For this reason, it is the definition which is most prevalent today, as is also indicated by the term used to describe social, economic, and political consolidation in a state, namely nation-building. But this term also obfuscates the reality faced by the citizen today. He is more often than not engaged in state-building rather than nation-building.

The confusion around the term nation-building, as Walker Connor has pointed out,[12] stems not only from a problem of semantics, but also from an ethnocentrism bound by an historical legacy. Nation-building is an American concept designed to characterize the process of consolidation in the United States since the revolt of the thirteen British colonies and the Declaration of Independence. Paradoxically, the immigrants who have forged the American community were often themselves victims of the excesses of nationalism and came to the New World to escape just that. Somehow, they did not avoid the terminology and conceptualization of the Old World and the rather American concepts of melting-pot and nation-building became ways of expressing the desires of many Americans to create a nation that would be better, stronger, and greater than the nations they had left behind. It was then assumed that the same process was going on elsewhere in the world.

But the coming into being of the idea of nation, though definitely bound with the growth of the activities of the state, did not always lead to the fusion of the nation with the state. The Dominions of the British Empire point to a contrary phenomenon where English-speaking Canadians, South Africans, Australians, and New Zealanders felt greater loyalty to the Crown and Westminster than to their own country and state. Furthermore, English Canadians seemed to express some difficulty in articulating what one might call Canadian nationalism. As John Holmes wrote: "In the pseudo-sophistication of our adolescence, many Canadians would rather let the country fall apart than be accused of nationalism, a weakness not only malign but also corny. Some find pride in our having conceived the immaculate non-nation."[13]

Many cohesive communities in the world today, be they big or small, expect nevertheless to be defined and accepted as nations. Some still demand that they be allowed to create their own state and thus remain in the main stream of the history of nationalism. Other communities have élites articulating demands that do not lead to the creation of a nation-state, but rather to a restructuration of the state in which they live.[14] These communities also define themselves as nations because this definition best expresses the need of the community for self-affirmation but the state to which they belong is not threatened with dislocation. The citizen ends up having a double loyalty, to his nation and to the state. This is generally the case in bi- or multinational states. Then there are communities which cannot be strictly defined as nations, but which, by their demands for greater recognition and participation in state activities, lead to the redefinition of the role of the state. These communities are known in Canada and the United States as ethnic groups.[15] As a result the state plays an important role not only in the opportunity for the self-affirmation of its nations and groups, but also in the relations between them. The state is in fact the arbiter of all community relations, whether they are defined as national, ethnic, or cultural. It is to the role of the state that we now turn.

The crucial role of the state is best understood by the possible outcomes of the relations between communities within it, be they nations, tribes, clans, or ethnic groups. Benjamin Akzin, in his brilliant essay *State and Nation*, suggests that there are three possible outcomes: integration, pluralism on the basis of inequality, and pluralism on the basis of equality. Let us look at each one of these outcomes.

The integrationist pattern can take place along two lines. The first is the assimilation of the numerically smaller communities into the numerically larger one. The latter will generally control the state, have political and economic power, and thereby encourage the assimilation of other communities by both overt and covert means. This is nation-building in the truest sense of the word. If need be, coercion will also be used to achieve this end. The other variation on the integrational pattern is the amalgamation of all communities into a new one which does not exhibit the characteristics of any of the earlier ones. This is a process that generally requires several

37

generations. A now commonly forgotten fact is that the Fathers of Confederation in Canada were thinking along such lines in the 1860s. Sir Georges Etienne Cartier, who coined the term of a new political nationality, said in 1865: "Now when we were united together, if union were attained, we would form a political nationality with which neither the national origin, nor the religion of any individual would interfere."[16] More than a century later, Canada is nowhere near having achieved this new political nationality.

It is the two pluralistic outcomes that have a better chance of success in the present-day world. Pluralism on the basis of inequality is generally dictated by the desires of the majority community to maintain its higher status in the state while giving some recognition to minority communities in order to forestall demands that could upset the status quo. It is not a policy that can be maintained very long and might in the end provoke demands by the minority communities or else their expulsion or even elimination if the dominant community feels threatened. Pluralism on the basis of equality, on the other hand, allows for all communities to participate in the running of the state and its social, economic, and political life. The important factor here is the ideological orientation of state institutions, as Azkin writes: "A bi- or multi-national State in this sense would be one in which prevailing State policy, rather than regarding the State as embodiment of a single nationality, of its culture and inherited values, regards the State's connection with two or more national cultures as equally intimate."[17] There are various constitutional options that make such an arrangement possible, but they need not concern us here.

These theoretical and historical considerations were necessary in order to determine whether the juxtaposition of cultural diversity and Canadian unity is contradictory. We contend that it is not contradictory and are in fact suggesting that it is politically imperative to recognize the link between cultural diversity and Canadian unity.

The image of the Canadian federation one gets today is not one where a fusion of nation and state has taken place, nor one where the state considers its connection with the various communities within Canada as equally intimate, to use Azkin's term. Let us first see why there has not been a fusion of nation and state. In 1867, Canada adopted the British parliamentary system and the majority of its population, for the better part of the first century of Canada's

Confederation, wholeheartedly identified with the *Pax Britannica* and British culture. But the political life of this country has moved away from the British political and cultural model since the end of the Second World War. Furthermore, there developed a double challenge to our federal system, one coming from the national demands of the Québécois, the other from the provinces. The result is a situation that signifies in effect that Canadians must re-think their political system.

Both challenges point to the difficulty of fusing nation and state in Canada. This is certainly clear from the Québécois challenge, both in the separatist and federalist versions. For many Québécois, the identification with the rest of Canada has not been an easy one, as René Lévesque points out: "Each time that I left Québec to travel in the other provinces — and I must point out that in those years, it happened more frequently than today — I had the impression of going to a foreign country where my language was not welcomed, where my way of seeing things, where my way of working 'clashed. . . .' "[18] As a result of such perceptions and experiences some Québécois have opted for the sovereignty and independence of Québec, while others argue for a new federal system where Québec and the Québécois would identify with and partake fully and equally with English-speaking Canadians in the activities of the Canadian federal state.

The challenge from the provinces reflects on the other hand, the unhappiness of English-speaking Canadians with the role and activities of the federal government. Whereas part of this reaction stems from the Québécois challenge, it is also the result of the feeling of many Canadians that their province, rather than the federal government, best responds to their needs. Although there is no rejection of the concept of Canada, there is nevertheless a challenge to Canadian unity. Even if the provincial challenge is often motivated by considerations of fiscal control and the claim by provincial politicians that they can better insure the development of their province and its people than Ottawa can, it still reflects a general malaise with federal policies. Furthermore, there are regional disagreements and perceptions that enter the debate and which are known well enough that they need not be repeated here.

These discordant notes on the federal scene have also ironically been enhanced by a policy of the Trudeau government whose intention was to encourage, rather than discourage, Canadian unity. It is the federal policy of multiculturalism. The Québécois have been the most openly opposed to the concept of multiculturalism in Canada. This is understandable in view of the intimate link they see between nation, nationalism, and culture. Furthermore they perceive that their own culture is thereby relegated to a folkloric manifestation. But this is neither inevitable nor logical. It is a perception that stems from their political experience in Canada, especially outside Québec. Canadians of Anglo-Saxon or Anglo-Celtic background are also known to reject this policy on the strength of the argument that Canada is an English-speaking country and that immigrants from other cultures ought simply to accept this fact and assimilate. The debates on this issue thus further strengthen the feeling that there is more than one perception of Canada. It must be noted, however, that despite the opposition to multiculturalism, many provinces have agreed to encourage and foster the original cultures of their citizens. Paradoxically, multiculturalism at the provincial level does not seem to bring about the objections and divisions perceptible at the federal level.

The present situation in this country easily leads one to the conclusion that there is no fusion between nation and state in Canada. If we are to learn from history, especially from the history of nationalism, then we have to acknowledge that Canada's unity and survival cannot be predicated on such a 'fusion. This means that the Canadian state must accept the role of arbiter of community and individual needs, that it must make equally intimate the cultures and cultural manifestations of its citizens. The gradual abandonment by Anglo-Saxon or Anglo-Celtic Canadians of their "Britishness," the nationalism of the Québécois, and the cultural vitality of Canadians of all cultural backgrounds are the reality of Canada today. Although there is a myth and a reality to what is often termed Canada's "mosaic," as Erwin Kreutzweiser has pointed out, the acknowledgement of cultural diversity, the encouragement of its manifestations and mutual acceptance can give Canada the ideological orientation it seems to lack presently. As Kreutzweiser further points out, in his argument on the importance of oral traditions in fostering the Canadian mosaic: "If, as is commonly said, Canada's unity is in its diversity and its identity is in its multiplicity, then Canadian oral traditions must obviously be some composite of those traditions of the diverse elements. . . . Consequently, such traditions must, according to popular opinion, be constituent elements in Canadian culture, and be celebrated as such."[19] The state must not only acknowledge such a basis for Canadian unity, but encourage it.[20] New constitutional arrangements might as a result also be made more easily.

The alternative to an ideological orientation of pluralism on the basis of equality is the perceptible fusion of state and nation, certainly in Québec, and elsewhere where union with the United States is not desired. But this will be the failure of Canada, a country which history and geography have favoured to succeed in the experiment of cooperating communities. Our success can be a contribution to humanity; our example can help many states whose composition is also not mononational. That is the political imperative of Canadian unity and cultural diversity.

Notes

[1]   Boyd C. Shafer, *Nationalism* (New York, 1955), p. 197.
[2]   Carlton J. H. Hayes, *The Historical Evolution of Modern Nationalism* (New York, 1931), p. 300.
[3]   Shafer, p. 196.
[4]   Shafer, p. 201.
[5]   René Lévesque, *La Passion du Québec* (Montréal, 1978), p. 13.
[6]   Shafer, p. 205.
[7]   Robert H. Keyserlingk, "Hitler and German Nationalism Before 1933," *Canadian Review of Studies in Nationalism*, 5, No. 1 (1978), 24-44.
[8]   See Royal Institute of International Affairs, *Nationalism* (London, 1939), p. 339.
[9]   Shafer, p. 208.
[10]  Carlton J. H. Hayes, *Essays on Nationalism* (New York, 1926), p. 146.
[11]  Hans Kohn. *The Idea of Nationalism* (New York, 1960), p. 13.
[12]  Walter Connor, "Nation-Building or Nation-Destroying?" *World Politics*, 24, No. 3 (1972), 319-55.
[13]  John Holmes, "Nationalism in Canadian Foreign Policy" in *Nationalism in Canada*, ed. Peter Russel (Toronto, 1966), p. 205.
[14]  We have termed this process minority nationalism. See our "Le nationalisme minoritaire: le cas de la Tchécoslovaquie," *Canadian Journal of Political Science*, 7, No. 2 (1974), 248-67.
[15]  On the similarities and differences between nations and ethnic groups see Konstantin Symmons-Symonolewicz, "Ethnicity and Nationalism: Recent Literature and Its Theoretical Implications," *Canadian Review of Studies in Nationalism*, 4, No. 1 (1979), 98-102.
[16]  Quoted in Donald V. Smiley, *The Canadian Political Nationality* (Toronto,

1967), p. iii.

[17] Benjamin Akzin, *State and Nation* (London, 1964), p. 138.

[18] Lévesque, p. 38.

[19] Erwin Kreutzweiser, "Canada, a Mosaic?" *The Chelsea Journal*, 5, No. 4 (1979), 151.

[20] This is not an easy task by any means, as the policy of multiculturalism has shown. Part of the problem lies in the lack of an adequate conceptual formulation of the policy as well as the role of myths that have arisen since the federal government introduced the policy of multiculturalism in 1972. For an examination of these problems see Jean Burnet, "The Policy of Multiculturalism within a Bilingual Framework: A Stock-Taking," *Canadian Ethnic Studies*, 10, No. 2 (1978), 107-13; and by the same author, "Myths and Multiculturalism," *Canadian Journal of Education*, 4, No. 4 (1979), 43-58.

STANISLAV J. KIRSCHBAUM is an Associate Professor of Political Science at York University's bilingual Glendon College. He was born in Slovakia and earned degrees at the Universities of Ottawa, Toronto, and Paris. He has been Visiting Professor at l'Université de Montréal, and Exchange Professor at l'Université Laval. He has published extensively on East European politics and nationalism.

# Québec Separatism and Christianity: Or A Highly Successful Cultural Pluralism: 2,000 Years of Roman Christianity

The ghost of separatism is upon us.

It has come out of a Québec clothes-closet. That closet is not one of the important ones, it is somewhere in the darkest corner of the basement.

What will happen now, I do not know. Can the ghost be chased back into its closet if we preach it a good lesson?

By all means, this is how I reason things out. Here is my syllogism:

1. To divide or separate what is united is not a Christian idea.

2. The French-Canadian people in Québec are a profoundly Christian one.

3. Therefore, if separation haunts Québec, it did not originate in the Christian ideology.

Let us examine these three propositions.

*Proposition 1*: To divide or separate what is united is not a Christian idea.

Christians believe that the cornerstone of everything is God.

Man's destiny is in God. And his life on this planet is but a small part of the full eternal life he is called to. The only real goal of full social happiness of mankind has to be set in the hereafter, for man is mortal in his body but his soul is immortal. It will live on in Heaven, and that is where exists even today the only perfect reality of a pluralistic society, the most adequate model of it being Christianity, under the condition that it be lived and experienced integrally.

During his stay on earth, how does man prepare for the eternal venture? God himself gave him the necessary instructions. They are in the Bible, principally in the New Testament. Speaking to all mankind, Jesus said: "Thou shalt love the Lord thy God with thy whole heart, and with thy whole soul, and with thy whole mind. This is the greatest and the first commandment. And the second is like it: 'Thou shalt love thy neighbour as thyself.' " That is not all. Jesus binds commandments 1 and 2 in something like a nearly mathematical equation: "A new commandment I give you, that you love one another: that as I loved you, you also love one another." We have here as much a set of laws as any in the field of scientific reality, such as universal gravity. And it is the very core of Christianism.

This set of laws alone explains the historic development of Christianity.

From the very first days they appeared in Palestine, the Christians grew in numbers, in spite of man's inner resistance to spiritual elevation out of pride and sensualism, and in spite of outside persecutions. The Roman Empire fell, and ever since, ideologies and political systems have emerged, waned, and disappeared. Christianity went on, growing statistically and in measurable achievements, both material and spiritual, becoming a masterpiece of pluralistic unity. (But why do many so easily belittle and despise the Middle Ages, when they were the time of a unified Europe under the Christian monarchies of the Western Empire, then the Holy Roman Empire?)

In time, opposition materialized in forceful philosophies and social theories of all sorts. The Christian Church became the target of many converging hostile intentions and resourceful strategies. So powerful did they become, they divided Christianity itself in various factions: those of the Oriental Schisms, those of Protestantism. That Christianity survived these inner crises is proof of its indestructibility founded on solid ground: the love of one God and his Christ; for even divided the Christians have the same unifying faith in Christ. That

Christianity survived at all is unique for an institution in world history.

Then it spread out from Europe to the world: it was the era of its missionary mystique. Continent after continent was, so to speak, invaded and welcomed in the Christian faith, which has now developed into the most important socio-religious phenomenon ever.

A united world is basically a Christian concept and ideal.

*Propostion* 2: The French-Canadian people in Québec are a profoundly Christian one.

It is an historical fact that New France was founded mainly by Catholic men and women, who led heroic lives in Ville-Marie from its very first years, building churches and convents, hospitals and schools for the French and the Indians, both sons and daughters of God. Sacrifices beyond belief have they accepted, even unto martyrdom, to render more effective their work in their Lord's vineyard.

But the test of Christianity in New France is not limited to those beginnings. In 1760, when the French-Canadians were defeated in Québec City by the English, and, left to themselves, came under British rule, they had to face a crucial situation. Would they survive as a Catholic community, praying to God in the language and culture which were theirs? They were 60,000 asking this question. In the 1960s, 200 years later, they were 6,000,000 living with the answer that had been given by their ancestors and the Church. For the Church had taken up the challenge. Most historians have expressed the opinion that without its profound and dynamic Catholicism, embodied in the Roman Church's hierarchical and social structure, Québec would not be Québec, that is the historic Québec — the one that has been traditionally the same up to about 1960.

Do we not all have in mind the panorama of a twentieth century Catholic Québec, practically the same as ever? A steeple in every town and village, and in the cities on practically every third street-corner; priests and nuns and brothers still building and directing churches, convents, hospitals, schools, giving their lives to their people and leading them on the high road of a religious community life, every aspect of that life, ideological, cultural, social, even economical and political, permeated with the religious faith dominating the land. One need not go on. This life of a nation is the mirror reflection of the very life of the church and its spirit. (Both have their achievements and their shortcomings — as there always are of both in any human endeavour.) Christianity does not claim perfection on earth, but it does claim it has received from God, with the guarantee this perfection exists in the other world, a safe road map leading to it.

*Proposition 3*: Therefore if separatism haunts Québec, it did not originate in the Christian ideology.

Québec is changing radically since 1960, when began what was deceitfully called "la révolution tranquille." (For instance, we know how directly the Catholic religion, its very heart, has been assaulted and corrupted, especially in the the key area of its school system.)

Presently, dark forces of Marxist allegiance are scuttling the ship that had survived many tempests. It would be too vast a task to get at the inner workings of the Québec revolution, but a few words on the world revolution will make things clearer.

World revolution stems from Modernism, a new name for an age-old virus of humanity.

The tree of Modernism as it evolved, has culminated in two main branches, affecting the way of life of all of us.

The first branch is man's natural egoistic individualism, outrageously masquerading as total-respect-of-one's-freedom. Everyone fends for himself and couldn't care less about others. Has it not got at the root of the otherwise highly productive free systems (political and economical) of the Western World?

The second branch is atheistic materialism, which as its only possible fruit could beget pragmatically oriented Marxist-communist socialism.

The American theologian, Vincent Miceli, in his important book *The Gods of Atheism* (by which title he means the atheists do have their gods notwithstanding their declarations to the contrary), writes: "Just as love of God creates a community of lovers of God so too hatred of God moves to create a community of haters of God" (p. 459). Further he writes: "There is therefore, a profound, metaphysical, logical and anti-social drive in every form of open or hidden atheism" (p. 460). And still further: "Atheist humanism in cutting man off from Communion with God also isolates him from his fellow man" (p. 464). It is obvious we are here at the antipodes of the Christian doctrine. We are here at the roots of revolution which aims at obtaining totalitarian control through the dynamics of brute force, terrorism, and the like.

Communism, as is shown in all literature pertaining to its strategic advance through world history, aims at world domination. It intends to unite the world in equal distribution of earthly goods and in material peace. It claims it will do so by revolution and psychological warfare. Its goal is on this earth exclusively. It is not haphazardly that it has been said that Communism is Christianity "gone mad" — in this sense that it mocks true unity of mankind, which it seeks by the wrong means.

Separatism is one of these means — I mean all separatisms and divisions, and they are numerous on our planet, today.

My syllogism has brought us to this point. Now may I ask: Can we not see clearly how it is that Christianity might be the only hoped for model of cultural pluralistic society we need? Undoubtedly, I speak as a Christian, for I am one and speak as such for myself as well as in the name of hundreds of millions who have the same faith.

Can we not say that under the attacks of powerfully atheistic and materialistic ideologies, Christianity, which is a fourth of the world population, keeps holding the fort? Unceasingly, the Roman Catholic Church introduces itself officially as "one, holy, catholic [that is universal], and apostolic [that is united by its head the Pope, successor of the apostles]," thereby setting itself as a working model of world unity.

We have seen how the Church's head spokesman has during the past year taken in hand the reigns of spiritual leadership in a disturbed world. John Paul II's first words after his election in the fall of 1978 were: "Brothers, Sisters, do not be afraid to welcome Christ and to accept his power! Do not be afraid! Christ knows 'what there is in man,' and he alone knows! Let Christ speak to man. He alone has the words of life, yes, of life everlasting!" In his October 18, 1978, address before an audience of diplomats, he said: "As a Christian, and still more as Pope, we are and will be witness of an universal love."

Then the Pope began to travel, as Saint Paul of the primitive church, and as becomes obvious no Pope will have done to this day. Everywhere, in Mexico, Poland, Ireland, and the United States, and to all, he has preached the Christian model of religious, ideological, and social life, with the respect and freedom due it from the political level.

The image he builds of Christianity is simple and bright. All are united in one faith, having the same destiny of peace and harmony in this world and of eternal happiness in the other world. All united, though diversified, and standing there, not looking at each other, in a flat, horizontal, pancake pattern, but together looking up to the same Pope, and beyond him, at his very beckoning, to the one and only Christ.

I will not quote a single line from the Pope's dozens of speeches and homilies the world has been an audience to. But I would add the Holy Father would not speak differently were he to come to Canada.

But then there is here in Canada, in Québec, an official extension of the Holy See, the Bishops of the Roman Church. They are well aware of the Québec problem. How do they deal with it? A quick look at the past will give us a springboard.

All through the history of Québec the Church hierarchy has steadfastly kept the tradition of Christian social unity and harmony. It never swayed in its policy of allegiance to the political authority: it actually helped to maintain the French Canadians in peace with their British masters (by victory and treaty). Nor did the hierarchy ever take sides with the Revolutionaries, in whatever conflict, as that of 1837, and the others that followed as well in Québec as in Western Canada. I will go a step further and say that the English-speaking and Protestant minorities of Québec are indebted principally to the Church for the freedom that has always been granted them with regard to language and religion, whereas the French-speaking minorities outside of Québec were not till very recently granted the equivalent.

And today, how do things stand? The Church has been, so to speak, side-tracked, and lay powers are running the railroad station. Still, the Church stands in confrontation with the mounting revolutionary elements. To demonstrate this would be lengthy and tedious. I will cut short, referring directly to one of the latest documents released by the Assembly of the Bishops of Québec: *The people of Québec and their political future.* (The English version not being available yet, I will translate a few excerpts from it.)

The gist of the Bishop's pastoral message is that there is a distinction to be made between national unity and political unity, that is to say, what makes up the national unity of the French-speaking population of Québec is not what constitutes the political unity of this same geographically enclosed entity. The Bishops here seem to refer to a section of Pope Pius XII's Christmas message of 1954, where he declares: "At its basis the error consists in confusing national life in its proper meaning and nationalist policy; the first, being the right and glory of a people, must be developed, the second, source of endless ills, must be rejected forcibly. . . . "

At one point the Bishops close a discussion with the conclusion: "By all means, Québec must never forget that interdependence is a condition common to all modern nations and that it could not reject all relations with its neighbors."

Further we read this highly meaningful rule of conduct given to the historically Roman Catholic people of Québec: "If one here is dealing with a people seeking better relationships, then Christians surely have a service to render and responsibilities to take."

One feels that the bishops of Québec, as is true also of Pope John Paul II, speak not to one nation or to four nations, nor to the nations of a time in history. The Church speaks out from above, so to speak, and with authority for all nations of all times. Theirs is a universal view, that can only be gotten from the high viewpoint of Revelation itself.

It is not surprising, then, that the continuity of the Christian dynamic concept of a cultural pluralism and their effective and iluminating simplicity, become more and more impressive as centuries roll by, and take on the vivid dimensions of a model.

LEO A. BRODEUR, native of Manitoba, has been in Québec for some 20 years. He has a Ph.D. from Laval University (1968) and is Full Professor at the University of Sherbrooke. He is founder of various research groups, two of which are of international scope, editor of three magazines, and specializes in teaching the Francophone Literatures and Semiotics. He has travelled extensively abroad, in Europe and on the African Continent, has published his doctoral thesis (*Le corps-sphère, clef de la symbolique claudélienne*) and various articles, and translations (prose and poetry). Founder-director of a publishing house, vice-president of the Canadian International Academy of Humanities and Social Sciences, he has received some ten research grants as individual researcher and as past director of CELEF (University of Sherbrooke).

# A Humane Look at the Unity Question

## Johnny Lombardi

It could be a very useful exercise if one were to approach solutions to our current concerns about the Canadian Unity question, by reviewing the direction our history has taken from the beginnings of Canada as a land, to today's Canada as a nation. Some may wish to argue that is quite sufficient to examine today's realities as we see them and set a course for future action. History, they say, is a useless remnant of an old past and of no use to anyone. Others may take the view, like I do, that historical facts provide a kind of record of human activity, a method of analyzing the past so that we can understand the present. In understanding the present, it will be easier to anticipate and plan the future. So, before we seek an answer to what is appropriate for Canada from the point of view of its pluralism of peoples and its unity as a country, let us take a brief look at human activity that has preceded us. Bear in mind, however, that this will by no means be the complete story or the only considerations to be reviewed. While the scientitst can examine an atom and predict exactly how another atom will behave, the same cannot be done with people. It was the British historian, G. M. Trevelyan, who said, "The life history of one man, or even of many individual men, will not tell you the life history of other men. Men are too complicated, too spiritual, too various, for a scientific analysis."

As we go back in time, it is difficult to locate any record of what must have been the first meeting between the original inhabitants of this land and Europeans on voyages of discovery to Canada. The Indians did not keep records, and evidence of pre-Columbus encounters are sketchy. Evidence has shown, however, that the Vikings were the first Europeans to set foot on Canadian soil, and yet there are myths and legends that Irish monks may have arrived 500 years earlier. We can mention many names from history, like Columbus, Cabot, Frobisher, and Hudson, but few people realize that it was a Portuguese explorer, Gaspar Corté Real, who named Cape Bonavista in Newfoundland. At any rate, both England and France in the sixteenth century competed for land and possible riches in what was then called the New World. The first Canadians, who were the Indians, must have looked out, seen the landing of the first explorers, and said, "Good, we need the tourist business," not realizing that in time, fierce battles would be fought over land and furs. But in looking closer at the human element, what we find is that the interaction of the Indians, French, and English produced a blending of cultures. The Indians taught the Europeans survival skills, such as canoeing, and were glad to get from the white men iron tools and weapons, metal pots and pans. In exchange the newcomer was glad to learn from the experience of the Indian how to adapt his clothing to the needs of the weather. There is no doubt that the lifestyle of the Indian was improved, but not without some negative effects. The white man brought with him diseases like smallpox and measles to the natives, plus alcohol and guns.

Slow beginnings, and gradual and frequently interrupted progress, marked the history of early French settlement in Canada. New France, as it was called, failed to attract immigrants in as large quantities as did the English settlement. However, between the early 1600s and the 1750s, the population had grown to about 60,000. During the 150 years as a French colony, New France developed strong roots and its own French-Canadian culture. This culture was knitted together through language, government, church, and family. In those days the Church was really several institutions in one. It provided religious guidance to both the Indians and the colony. It was influential in government, and provided schooling, hospitals, and charity.

New France, however, did come under British control, but only through long struggles between empires. It began with the fur traders and ended in military fashion when the British Army took control in 1760. One must remember that England and France had fought each other in Europe for centuries. The conflicts simply spilled over into the colonies established in Canada. Let us examine the effects the British takeover had on the French Canadians. "New France" had been very dependent on the mother country throughout its existence. France had supplied its rulers, its educators, and its priests. "If the French Canadians were to remain French," as historian Mason Wade puts it, "they had to do so on the strength of their own resources, under . . . a foreign power whose religion, language, laws and customs were very different from their own." They quite naturally, over the years that followed, developed a sense of inferiority. Under the domination of the English, they fell to a lowly position. This is where the nucleus of the present discontent stems. Keep this point in mind. For in it could lay the part-solution to the Canadian Unity question.

What we have learned from history indicates that the more the French *feel* that their growth and cultural individualism are stifled, the more they will strive to achieve their goal. Today's French Canadians of the separatist movement seem to be fired with an enthusiasm to be a "free" people, in the context of their ancestors' definition of freedom; that is to say, that throughout their generations they have felt overpowered, outnumbered, and overburdened by British policies which were influenced by the manners, customs, and traditions of the Mother Country.

Looking at the problem from a human level, any student of history can observe that the French separatist element is emotionally reacting to having been the underdog for all these generations. The Canada of today is a far cry from the Canada of yesterday. The facts are that a policy of bilingualism exists; Confederation is a reality. Another reality is the cultural pluralism that is reflected in Canadian society today. Canada has developed into the great country that it is as a result of immigration, which since Confederation has seen the growth of smaller minorities, of nationalities other than French and English. An interesting statistic that the French would be quick to point out, is that Britain continues to be the major source country of immigrants with other large groups coming from the United States. The French would look at the fact that these latter-day immigrants who have contributed to cultural pluralism were not here as the founding nation, nor are they descendants of those pre-Confederation pioneers. They would dismiss the point as having no merit.

Conclusions: It is fair to say that any movement which seeks to steer away from the principles of brotherly love, unselfish acts for humanity, and love for mankind is a backward step. It will also be a backward step for Canadians to allow the breakup of this country; for the future of planet earth, if it is to continue to develop and grow in peace, must do so not in isolation of one country or one people from another, but in harmony and cooperative support. Canadians must do everything possible to prevent this potential split from occuring, short of taking up arms, or engaging in any kind of violence or abusive conduct. If French Canadians are to be convinced that to separate will be a backward step, then a massive campaign has to be launched aimed at convincing the French that the rest of Canada would be sorry to see them leave — not for selfish reasons, but because they are as much Canadian as the English and other minorities. Love and concern are the only weapons which will be effective against their emotional disposition over the issue of separating. This is not to say that the solution will be as simplistic as that tends to suggest, but if properly approached, could provide just the stimulus needed for a dialogue which can lead to the mechanics and practicalities of a closer cultural association — an association which will promote the image of pride in the two cultures, co-existing within the pluralistic whole, rather than an image of indifferent tolerance, bearing in mind that the root cause of the dichotomy is the sense of inferiority which has stemmed unabated from the 1700s.

But time is running out. A massive education campaign and a love campaign should be embarked on, that will touch the average person on both sides of the fence — the one in English Canada who does not know French history nor understand the culture, and the one in French Canada who feels that there is a big bad, impatient wolf outside the boundary of Québec.

Indeed, the whole question of Canadian Unity has intensified the negative mental thoughts and attitudes of people on both sides, like a silent hatred projected to each other. The sooner these thought patterns can be replaced by mental attitudes of love, the better, for it is a proven fact of the science of parapsychology that the tangible effects of such thought patterns are real. If and when the Referendum is to take place, that will be the final arbiter on what the majority of French

Canadians want. If we believe in a free country and the principles of freedom, we must accept the results of the democratic process. If the process proves that some form of separation is the wish of the majority, then let it be negotiated.

It is only a caged bird that wants to escape.

The real test could very well be *our* test. If *we* still love the French at that point, we will let them be free.

This paper has not dealt with the problem from the standpoint of the mechanics or the machinery of government, business, statutes, etc. It has only sought to investigate the source of the problem so that the source, once isolated, can be attended to.


JOHNNY LOMBARDI is President of North America's unique multicultural radio station, CHIN AM/FM, broadcasting in over thirty languages. Born in downtown Toronto in 1918 of Italian parents, he joined the army, and has presented international concerts at leading theatres in North America. On November 3, 1977, he was one of two recipients of the Canadian Family of Man Awards, highest citation bestowed by the League for Human Rights of B'nai B'rith of Canada.

# The Canadian Polish Community
# in the Light of the 1976 Census Results

Rudolf K. Kogler

Three measures used in the Canadian Census of Population could be applied to observe changes in the ethnocultural make-up of Canada:

1. *Ethnic Origin*, in response to the question: "to which ethnic or cultural group did you or your ancestor (on the male side) belong on coming to this continent?"
2. *Mother Tongue*, in response to the question: "language first spoken and still understood?"
3. *Language spoken at home*, in response to the question: "what language do you most often speak at home now?"

The analysis of these questions allows us to observe changes occurring within various ethnic groups, both within a purely demographic context, such as age and sex composition, geographic distribution, etc., as well as the degree of assimilation into dominant group or groups.

The most loosely defined concept of ethnicity and the one most often used by spokesmen of various ethnocultural groups are data obtained in response to the question about "Ethnic Origin." In reality, however, data shown under the heading "ethnic origin" do not reflect the real size of a given group, since the correlation between what is understood by "ethnic origin" and the actual sense of "belonging" to a particular language group is quite tenuous. In ethnic studies the data under the heading "ethnic origin" are useful when cross-classified with the other two criteria: "mother tongue" and "language spoken at home," since they enable us to gauge the degree of assimilation into the dominant group. Let us remember that the census questionnaire does not provide the opportunity to replay "Canadian" to the question on ethnicity. In these circumstances, respondents have to identify their ethnic background as: English, French, German, Polish, etc. If there were a possibility to answer "Canadian" to the first question, the statistical profile of ethnic groups in Canada would be different.

The most useful description of ethnic identification appears to be the "Mother Tongue." The information obtained in response to the question on the respondent's ethnic background is too imprecise since it is open to subjective interpretation. Members of the Canadian Polish Institute, in their papers and articles, have brought attention to this fact in discussing "inter-ethnic transfers."

On the other hand, the responses to the question "language most often spoken at home" give a much too narrow interpretation, eliminating such situations as: mixed marriages, and the second and third generation descendents of immigrants, who frequently possess some knowledge of their "mother tongue" but not enough to use it in a normal conversation. Although they do not possess the language skills, they have a great appreciation for the culture of their ancestors and a strong affinity for their ethnic group.

In this situation the "mother tongue" question can be regarded as the best medium for assessing the real strength of respective ethnic groups, eliminating most ambiguities of the other two questions. However, one should be cautious while interpreting the responses to that question, since they do not provide us with answer as to what language is presently used at home. Respondents by providing a given language as "mother tongue" could possibly use another language in everyday life. They could have been using "mother tongue" several years ago and still understand it but not use it in their everyday activities. As a result, data obtained from the question on "mother tongue" could either underestimate or overestimate the actual size of a particular ethnic group.

Questions pertaining to ethno-cultural identity are asked in the decennial census. The quinquennial census is of more limited scope, and asks questions only on the most important matters in order to assess the size and distribution of the Canadian population and its demographic profile. In 1976, for the first time, the question on "mother tongue" was introduced which in the past appeared only in the decennial census. It is a significant decision.

Let us now turn to the 1976 census and review data pertaining to the Polish ethnic group in relation to changes which occurred (1) inside the group and (2) in comparison to other groups forming the Canadian mosaic.

In June 1976, 99,855 people declared that they know or have knowledge of the Polish language. It is the lowest number since 1941. Table 1 illustrates this point.

The decline from 1961, when the number using the Polish language as their "mother tongue" was the largest, to 1976, in absolute terms is 61,865 and in relative terms 38.3 per cent. In proportion to the total Canadian population the decrease amounts to 55.5 per cent. This table also indicates the quickening pace of the decrease. In the period between 1961-71 the decrease was 16.6 per cent (1.6 per cent per annum) but during the 1971-76 period the pace increased to 25.9 per cent or 4.7 per cent per annum.

Assuming that the rate of decline will not change, that is, it will continue at 5.0 per cent annually, *ceteris paribus*, then the number of people who know Polish in the year 2001 will amount to 28,000. If the rate of decline should double then the number of people who know Polish would amount to only 14,000 in 2001. Table 2 illustrates this point.

Scrutiny of Table 1, which shows the geographic distribution of those who know Polish, indicates that in the period between 1961-76 the greatest decline occurred in the Atlantic provinces, Manitoba, and Saskatchewan. The aggregate decline amounted to 52.2 per cent or 3.0 per cent per annum. We can assume that in those provinces by 2001, knowledge of the Polish language would practically disappear. Reasons for this situation are obvious: widely dispersed Polish population and lack of active Polish organizations and parishes. These factors speed up the pace of assimilation. In Alberta and Québec the rate of decline amounted to 41.5 per cent or 2.3 per cent annually; in British Columbia the decrease amounted to 36.9 per cent or 2.1 per cent annually. In Ontario the situation is better, since the decrease is only 31.4 per cent or 1.8 per cent per annum. This comparatively good

## TABLE 1

### CANADA: DISTRIBUTION OF PERSONS WHO REPORTED THEIR "MOTHER TONGUE" AS POLISH, 1961, 1971 AND 1976

| PROVINCE | 1961 | 1971 | 1976 | CHANGE 1961-1971 NUMBER | PER CENT | 1971-1976 NUMBER | PER CENT | 1961-1976 NUMBER | PER CENT | DISTRIBUTION 1961 PER CENT | 1971 PER CENT | 1976 PER CENT |
|---|---|---|---|---|---|---|---|---|---|---|---|---|
| Newfoundland | 125 | 45 | 45 | -80 | -64.0 | 0 | 0 | -80 | -64.0 | 0.1 | 0.0 | 0.1 |
| Prince Edward Island | 46 | 40 | 35 | -6 | -13.0 | -5 | -12.5 | -11 | -23.9 | 0.0 | 0.0 | 0.0 |
| Nova Scotia | 1,053 | 555 | 420 | -498 | -47.3 | -135 | -24.3 | -633 | -60.1 | 0.6 | 0.4 | 0.4 |
| New Brunswick | 310 | 155 | 135 | -155 | -50.0 | -20 | -12.9 | -175 | -56.5 | 0.2 | 0.1 | 0.1 |
| Quebec | 19,827 | 15,480 | 11,680 | -4,347 | -21.9 | -3,800 | -24.5 | -8,147 | -41.1 | 12.3 | 11.5 | 11.7 |
| Ontario | 83,214 | 73,985 | 57,050 | -9,229 | -11.1 | -16,935 | -22.9 | -26,164 | -31.4 | 51.4 | 54.9 | 57.1 |
| Manitoba | 20,652 | 15,900 | 10,220 | -4,752 | -23.0 | -5,680 | -35.7 | -10,432 | -50.5 | 12.8 | 11.8 | 10.2 |
| Saskatchewan | 10,585 | 7,675 | 4,810 | -2,910 | -27.5 | -2,865 | -37.3 | -5,775 | -54.6 | 6.5 | 5.7 | 4.8 |
| Alberta | 16,755 | 13,725 | 9,735 | -3,030 | -18.1 | -3,990 | -29.1 | -7,020 | -41.9 | 10.4 | 10.2 | 9.8 |
| British Columbia | 8,978 | 7,105 | 5,665 | -1,873 | -20.9 | -1,440 | -20.3 | -3,313 | -36.9 | 5.5 | 5.3 | 5.7 |
| Yukon | 84 | 55 | 20 | -29 | -34.5 | -35 | -63.6 | -64 | -76.2 | 0.1 | 0.0 | 0.0 |
| Northwest Territories | 91 | 60 | 40 | -31 | -34.1 | -20 | -33.3 | -51 | -56.0 | 0.1 | 0.1 | 0.1 |
| Total | 161,720 | 134,780 | 99,855 | -26,940 | -16.6 | -34,925 | -25.9 | -61,865 | -38.3 | 100.0 | 100.0 | 100.0 |

TABLE 2

CANADA: POPULATION BY MOTHER TONGUE, 1961, 1971 AND 1976

| MOTHER TONGUE | 1961 | 1971 | 1976 | CHANGE | | | | | | DISTRIBUTION | | |
|---|---|---|---|---|---|---|---|---|---|---|---|---|
| | | | | 1961 - 1971 | | 1971 - 1976 | | 1961 - 1976 | | 1961 | 1971 | 1976 |
| | | | | NUMBER | PER CENT | NUMBER | PER CENT | NUMBER | PER CENT | PER CENT | PER CENT | PER CENT |
| English | 10,660,534 | 12,973,810 | 14,122,765 | 2,313,276 | 21.7 | 1,148,955 | 8.9 | 3,462,231 | 32.5 | 58.5 | 60.2 | 61.4 |
| French | 5,123,151 | 5,793,650 | 5,887,205 | 670,499 | 13.1 | 93,555 | 1.6 | 764,054 | 14.9 | 28.1 | 26.9 | 25.6 |
| Baltic languages (1) | 42,889 | 43,385 | 34,190 | 496 | 1.2 | -9,195 | -21.2 | -8,699 | -20.3 | 0.2 | 0.2 | 0.1 |
| Celtic languages (2) | M.A. | 24,360 | 10,060 | 24,360 | - | -14,300 | -58.7 | 10,060 | - | M.A. | 0.1 | 0.1 |
| Chinese and Japanese | 66,955 | 111,750 | 148,090 | 44,795 | 66.9 | 36,340 | 32.5 | 81,135 | 121.2 | 0.4 | 0.5 | 0.6 |
| Czech and Slovak | 42,546 | 45,145 | 34,955 | 2,599 | 6.1 | -10,190 | -22.6 | -7,591 | -17.8 | 0.2 | 0.2 | 0.2 |
| Dutch and Flemish | 184,481 | 159,165 | 122,555 | -25,316 | -13.7 | -36,610 | -23.0 | -61,926 | -33.6 | 1.0 | 0.7 | 0.5 |
| German | 563,713 | 561,085 | 476,715 | -2,628 | -0.5 | -84,370 | -15.0 | -86,998 | -15.4 | 3.1 | 2.6 | 2.1 |
| Greek | 40,455 | 104,455 | 91,530 | 64,000 | 158.2 | -12,925 | -12.4 | 51,075 | 126.3 | 0.2 | 0.5 | 0.4 |
| Hungarian | 85,939 | 86,835 | 69,305 | 896 | 1.0 | -17,530 | -20.2 | -16,634 | -19.4 | 0.5 | 0.4 | 0.3 |
| Indian and Eskimo | 166,531 | 179,820 | 133,010 | 13,289 | 8.0 | -46,810 | -26.0 | -33,521 | -20.1 | 0.9 | 0.8 | 0.6 |
| Indo-Pakistani | 4,505 | 32,555 | 58,420 | 28,050 | 622.6 | 25,865 | 79.5 | 53,915 | 1,196.8 | 0.0 | 0.2 | 0.3 |
| Italian | 339,626 | 538,360 | 484,045 | 198,734 | 58.5 | -54,315 | -10.0 | 144,419 | 42.5 | 1.9 | 2.5 | 2.1 |
| Polish | 161,720 | 134,780 | 99,865 | -26,940 | -16.6 | -34,935 | -25.9 | -61,875 | -38.3 | 0.9 | 0.6 | 0.4 |
| Portuguese | 18,213 | 86,925 | 126,535 | 68,712 | 377.3 | 39,610 | 45.6 | 108,322 | 594.8 | 0.1 | 0.4 | 0.6 |
| Russian | 42,903 | 31,745 | 23,480 | -11,158 | -26.0 | -8,265 | -26.0 | -19,423 | -45.3 | 0.2 | 0.1 | 0.1 |
| Scandinavian | 116,714 | 84,335 | 59,410 | -32,379 | -27.7 | -24,925 | -29.6 | -57,304 | -49.1 | 0.6 | 0.4 | 0.3 |
| Spanish | 6,720 | 23,815 | 44,130 | 17,095 | 254.4 | 20,315 | 85.3 | 37,410 | 556.7 | 0.0 | 0.1 | 0.2 |
| Ukrainian | 361,496 | 309,855 | 282,060 | -51,641 | -14.3 | -27,795 | -9.0 | -79,436 | -22.0 | 2.0 | 1.5 | 1.2 |
| Yiddish | 82,448 | 49,890 | 23,440 | -32,558 | -39.5 | -26,450 | -53.0 | -59,008 | -71.6 | 0.5 | 0.2 | 0.1 |
| Yugoslav languages (3) | 28,866 | 74,190 | 77,570 | 45,324 | 157.0 | 3,380 | 4.6 | 48,704 | 168.7 | 0.2 | 0.3 | 0.3 |
| Other | 97,842 | 118,410 | 138,270 | 20,568 | 21.0 | 19,860 | 16.8 | 40,428 | 41.3 | 0.5 | 0.6 | 0.6 |
| Not stated | - | - | 445,020 | - | - | 445,020 | - | 445,020 | - | - | - | 1.9 |
| Total | 18,238,247 | 21,568,320 | 22,992,605 | 3,330,073 | 18.3 | 1,424,285 | 6.6 | 4,754,358 | 26.1 | 100.0 | 100.0 | 100.0 |

NOTE: (1) Estonian, Lettish and Lithuanian; (2) Gaelic, Welsh and other Celtic; (3) Croatian, Serbian, Slovenian and other Yugoslav languages.

showing is a result of (a) larger concentration of Polish people, (b) a large number of active organizations and parishes, and (c) the steady trickle of Polish immigrants who settle in Ontario. We can assume that by 2001, despite the steady decline of Polish speaking population, there would remain in Ontario between 10,000 and 15,000 people who would understand Polish. Smaller concentrations will be found in Québec, Alberta, and British Columbia.

Table 2 indicates the changes which took place in Canada during 1961-71 regarding the population classified by "mother tongue." In order to facilitate the analysis, the population of Canada was divided into 22 language groups. The largest increases occurred in the following groups:

Indo-Pakistani .............................. twelvefold
Portuguese ................................... sixfold
Spanish ..................................... fivefold
Yugoslav ................................... threefold
Greek ................................. 126.0 per cent
Chinese and Japanese ................... 121.0 per cent

These increases resulted from the large influx of immigrants after the recent changes in immigration procedures. Eleven language groups sustained losses ranging from a high of 72.0 per cent for the Jewish group to 15.0 per cent for the German group. The number of Polish-speaking people fell by 38.0 per cent which puts this group in fourth place on the scale of losses from the highest to the lowest.

The number of people who claim English as their "mother tongue" grew by 32.5 per cent, whereas those indicating French as their "mother tongue" grew only by 15.0 per cent.

Table 3 provides a more detailed analysis of the changes in the language profile of the Canadian population by taking into account natural increase and immigration during the last five years. Similar data for the period 1961-71 will be provided in the near future.

Scrutiny of Table 3 shows that only the English-language group grew by 5.2 per cent. The Portuguese-language group, as a result of a large influx of immigrants, did not suffer any losses, whereas *all* other (20 language groups) lost ground, ranging from 1.0 per cent for the French-language group to 60.0 per cent for the Celtic language group. The Polish-language group lost almost 30.0 per cent and took sixth

TABLE 3

CANADA: POPULATION BY MOTHER TONGUE, SHOWING COMPONENTS OF POPULATION CHANGE, 1971-1976

| LANGUAGE GROUP | POPULATION 1971 | NATURAL INCREASE | NET MIGRATION | EXPECTED POPULATION 1976 | CENSUS* 1976 | DIFFERENCE | |
|---|---|---|---|---|---|---|---|
| | | | | | | NUMBER | PER CENT |
| English | 12,973,810 | 563,255 | 188,352 | 13,725,417 | 14,404,724 | 679,307 | +5.2 |
| French | 5,793,650 | 251,530 | 15,110 | 6,060,290 | 6,001,151 | -59,139 | -1.0 |
| Baltic | 43,385 | 1,883 | 277 | 45,545 | 34,852 | -10,693 | -23.5 |
| Celtic | 24,360 | 1,058 | M.A. | 25,418 | 10,255 | -15,163 | -59.7 |
| Chinese and Japanese | 111,750 | 4,852 | 43,023 | 159,625 | 150,956 | -8,669 | -5.4 |
| Czech and Slovak | 45,145 | 1,960 | 1,121 | 48,226 | 35,632 | -12,594 | -26.1 |
| Dutch and Flemish | 159,165 | 6,910 | 4,632 | 170,707 | 124,927 | -45,780 | -26.8 |
| German | 561,085 | 24,360 | 9,153 | 594,598 | 485,942 | -108,656 | -18.3 |
| Greek | 104,455 | 4,535 | 14,522 | 123,512 | 93,302 | -30,210 | -24.5 |
| Hungarian | 86,835 | 3,769 | 2,017 | 92,621 | 70,646 | -21,975 | -23.7 |
| Indian and Eskimo | 179,820 | 7,807 | % | 187,627 | 135,584 | -52,043 | -27.7 |
| Indo-Pakistani | 32,555 | 1,413 | 45,614 | 79,582 | 59,551 | -20,031 | -25.2 |
| Italian | 538,360 | 23,373 | 15,512 | 577,245 | 493,414 | -83,831 | -14.5 |
| Polish | 134,780 | 5,851 | 4,223 | 144,854 | 101,777 | -43,077 | -29.7 |
| Portuguese | 86,925 | 3,774 | 38,285 | 128,984 | 128,984 | 0 | 0 |
| Russian | 31,745 | 1,378 | 1,233 | 34,356 | 23,934 | -10,422 | -30.3 |
| Scandinavian | 84,335 | 3,661 | 3,039 | 91,035 | 60,560 | -30,475 | -33.5 |
| Spanish | 23,815 | 1,034 | 44,736 | 69,585 | 44,984 | -24,601 | -35.4 |
| Ukrainian | 309,855 | 13,452 | 1,234 | 324,541 | 287,519 | -37,022 | -11.4 |
| Yiddish | 49,890 | 2,166 | 1,707 | 53,763 | 23,894 | -29,869 | -55.6 |
| Yugoslav | 74,190 | 3,221 | 9,886 | 87,297 | 79,071 | -8,226 | -9.4 |
| Other | 118,410 | 5,140 | 44,227 | 167,777 | 140,946 | -26,831 | -16.0 |
| Total | 21,568,320 | 936,382 | 487,903 | 22,992,605 | 22,992,605 | 0 | 0 |

*) Adjusted: category "not stated" distributed proportionally among Language Groups

place in the scale ranging from the highest to the lowest. In the Slavic-language group, which interests us most, the losses are:

Russian .............................. 30.3 per cent
Polish ................................ 29.7 per cent
Czech and Slovak ....................... 26.1 per cent
Ukranian .............................. 11.4 per cent
Yugoslav languages ..................... 9.4 per cent

The foregoing table shows a large disproportion of losses, from 30.0 per cent to 9.0 per cent. The losses of the Russian group can be explained by a lack of immigration, great dispersal, and the absence of a network of active organizations.

In comparison with the Russian language group, losses in the Ukranian language group were two-thirds less, even though the influx of immigrants to this group was just as small. The process of assimilation was retarded through intensive cultural programs, strong organizational links with increased influence emanating from cultural centres and institutions, as well as close co-operation between church and lay organizations.

In this context we should examine the rapid process of assimilation of the Polish-language group. The influx of immigrants, although small, was four times as great as that for the Ukranian group in absolute numbers. In relative terms it was much greater, since the ratio of Polish immigrants was 31 per 1,000 Polish population as compared to 4 per 1,000 Ukranian population. The Polish group is just as well organized, with a good network of organizations, cultural institutions, etc., except that the Polish church hierarchy is less involved in the life of Polish lay organizations. Furthermore, groups have better access to Polish books, newspapers, and periodicals published in Poland and abroad. For these reasons it might be imperative to study the causes of the accelerated assimilation of the Polish language group. This trend was also observed and commented upon by several researchers of other than Polish descent.

The relatively small losses of the Yugoslav language group reflect a large influx of immigrants in the past 10 years. We could speculate that in the future this group may also show some decline perhaps up to 3.0 per cent annually.

In conclusion, results from the 1976 census, shown in Table 3, put the efficacy of the Multicultural policies in some doubt. It is evident that all language groups, including the French group, lose the proficiency of their respective languages and acquire the dominant language. In some language groups the process of assimilation is slower, such as Ukranian, and in others the process is faster. This reflects the resilience of the particular language group.

RUDOLF K. KOGLER was born in 1919 in the town of Wadowice, Poland. He graduated from the local high school in 1938, joined the Polish Army, and took part in the Polish campaign. He left Poland in 1939 and joined the Polish Army operating in the Middle East. At the end of the war, he went to Great Britain and entered St. Andrew's University in Scotland where he obtained an M.A. degree in Economics and Psychology. He arrived in Toronto in 1952, worked for a private firm, and finally joined the Ontario Civil Service where he occupies at present the position of Chief of the Demographic Section. He has published several studies on the Polish Ethnic Group.

# On Multiculturalism as a Limit of Canadian Life

James N. Porter

## Introduction

The aim of this inquiry is to aid in the formulation of the idea of multiculturalism in a way that enables one to see the good it represents.[1] Our interest is to understand how and for whom multiculturalism could be attractive, and how and for whom it could be repulsive, so we want to imagine the kind of life that devotion to multiculturalism produces. Our aim is not to produce a description or definition of multiculturalism, for we do not wish to treat it as a thing to be possessed or ignored. Our aim is not to give information about it (as if there could be moral information), rather it is to invigorate and cultivate a moral problem — the problem of what it could mean to wish to live a multicultural life. We take it to be the case that multiculturalism as an idea wishes to be heard as a commitment to a particular version of a life worth living, a life that could be desired, that could inspire passion in both its friends and its enemies, a life to which it would be difficult to be indifferent. It is this committed character of the idea that seems to be referenced by its name — that it is an "ism." It is this that could cause the idea to be an embarrassment to objective thinkers, for they could never consider it except at some risk — the risk of being moved by the temptation to recognize multiculturalism as a desire and not as a thing.

Multiculturalism is not a fact: it is a theory or idea, a way of talking and thinking and acting in relation to cultural differences; it is a conception of the place and value of cultural differences. Part of understanding multiculturalism is seeing that its practices are not obviously one's own, seeing that there are other things one could do in relation to such differences. Our inquiry will try to hear what some of those other things could be through considering some examples of them; we do not presume that one ought to embrace multiculturalism or that Canada is, or ought be, or even could be a multiculturalist society. We want to know what the multicultural idea is.

## Multiculturalism and Culture

If the multicultural ideal is truly an ideal, truly a commitment, truly something that someone could care about or be interested in, then it must be something other than the expedient recognition that the Canadian state extends its rule over a population from different cultural backgrounds. This fact is not what we hear multiculturalism to be about. We hear it as a recommendation or bit of advice about how one ought to act in relation to this fact. Multiculturalism, then, is an interpretation of cultural difference, an interpretation contested by other interpretations. We suspect that how one interprets the fact of cultural multiplicity is a reflection of how one interprets cultural singularity, i.e., a reflection of what one takes culture itself to be in the first place. If one takes a given culture to be that which is in the first place, then cultural difference will occupy second place. If one takes one's own place as what is first, then the place of another is of secondary interest.

Typically, a culture is understood as the way of life of a people. But this is very abstract. Life, we wish to suggest, is lived particularly, and if a culture is a way of life, then culture is a particular way of doing particular things — not only a way of life, but also a way of death, and birth, a way of walking and dreaming and talking and eating and dressing, and the list is endless. But culture is more than just a list of individual practices: it is an organization of practices into institutions by communities, it is a particular history and tradition of life, of which any particular practice may be understood as representative. In this practical sense, there is no limit to a culture. From this perspective, the only limit to a culture is another culture. One culture ends where another begins. In this sense cultures represent particular homes for particular peoples, and one is only aware of being away from home when one comes to the place of a stranger. The stranger may invite me to "make myself at home," but the fact that I must *do* it shows me the difference between his home (where I must work to make my home) and my own home (where I can relax, enjoy the fruits of previous labours, and be at home naturally).

So a culture is a natural place, a place where one encounters familiar ways, i.e., ways like those of one's own family. A place of many cultures could, from this perspective, seem a foreign place — complex and always different from what one had expected. It would be a place where one encountered strangers — strange ways, strange sounds and smells — where one could not relax and be natural. One who could not relax and be natural in a place of different ways of living might be one who was always standing on guard. What would he or she be guarding? Probably the naturalness of a certain way of life. If so, then naturalness is seen to be threatened or inhibited by difference. This seems a curious state of affairs; how could it be? How could what is merely different — a different way of acting — be seen as threatening? Clearly it often is the case, as is demonstrated by both the daily facts of prejudice and bigotry and by the structural facts of immigration and educational policy, all of which seek to control difference and insure a certain similarity of conduct and background. Parallel impulses are at work in the very idea of law itself, wherein particular modes of conduct or particular acts are made punishable because in some way they threaten the ability of others to live undisturbed in a situation they take to be one of natural peacefulness. There is a sense, then, in which any culture represents a more or less strong, but always passionate, commitment to the preservation of particular usages and traditions of life — and every culture supports those ways through repressive punishments of deviations from its ways. Deviations are marked, through repression, as being outside the community. Deviation is representative of unwanted difference.

From this perspective, multiculturalism appears as a commitment to a strange reversal of the natural. Multiculturalism asks us to see the world differently — to see that the outside (difference) is inside (the community) and the inside (prejudice) is outside (deviance). Multiculturalism confuses natural clarity. Multiculturalism seems to be unnatural since it asks us to revise our conception of what is natural and what is good. Let us examine this peculiar request.

Multiculturalism seems to be a result of thinking about what is good, about the relation of human practices to their aim or end — to what unifies them — an idea of the reason for doing things in a particular way. The thinking that could have produced multiculturalism is a thinking that recognizes difference within every culture, e.g., the difference between what is done and why it is done. This thinking recognizes that every culture recognizes a difference between good and bad, and that the ways of every culture can be and are used for good and bad purposes.

The strength of a culture is its way of indicating its conception of a life worth living. How is this done? It is done by employing the usages of that culture — by using the familiar things and ideas and practices of the culture. These usages are thus resources that men and women employ in order to live as well as they can, and in order to show to themselves and to others what goodness is. Familiar usages are, in this employment, powerful resources. Their power is their ability to influence a person — not that they determine a person's conduct, but that they can be felt by a person as tempting (inviting or repulsive) and that he can therefore notice their effect upon him. The strength of a usage is its ability to suggest a difference between itself and what is good. A weak usage presents itself as good in itself and takes what is different from itself as bad. This is the weakness of what claims to be good, and the strength of what is not good.

From this perspective, multiculturalism seems to be an attempt to increase the range of familiar usages which a person can employ to influence himself and others. Multiculturalism wishes to enhance a person's capacity to act in relation to what is good. But multiculturalism presents *itself* as an image or example of what is good. What is its good? How is it not merely a morally neutral technique, or worse, an example of the weak usage that confuses itself with the good it represents? Within any particular culture the usages which are available to an actor have the appearance of being naturally available to her use, and the choices made are treated unreflectively, i.e., naturally. The multicultural society encourages (perhaps even forces) the actor to become responsible both for the usages she employs and for their employment. It makes the fact of her having made a choice obvious, i.e., her choices are no longer natural. The origin of conduct is no longer treated as nature, but as desire.

To employ usage more in the spirit of an example than as what is good in itself produces an ironic result: exclusive or possessive attachment to a particular usage becomes impossible, because that which one uses becomes an example of what one needs. What is needed is the difference that one makes between usage and the idea or purpose for which it is employed. Why is this difference needed? This difference is needed in order to preserve one's desire, i.e., to preserve the reason for acting in the first place. Hence multiculturalism's good is desire; multiculturalism is a strategy of commitment that sees the natural life of a single culture as insular, as cut off from the source of its own practice, where that source is the human desire that produces the practice. Multiculturalism seeks to enliven usage by treating it as an example of what is desirable rather than a thing that is desired. If it is only a thing, the best one can do with usage is discriminate or choose between better and poorer things. The discriminator is unironic — he acts as if what he chooses is good in itself. The discriminator sees no need for desire, he thinks he only needs to possess good things and avoid bad ones. The discriminator treats the world as a naturally existing array of good and bad things or practices or people. He does not cultivate his desire but merely exploits its natural abundance. The discriminator does not see the difference between inside and outside as a product of his desire; he treats this difference as natural, as what is first.

The fate of the discriminator is tragic. By this I mean that she is progressively isolated from the life she seeks to defend, which, because it is not cultivated, can only decay, wear out, and be worn down by its constant effort to insulate itself from being influenced. Perhaps this is why discriminators often appear as survivors of a lost cause. They seem to see that since what is good is what is first or original, and that since they are not first (but rather act in the name of what was first — in the name of the forefathers), that they are among the last, preserving an impulse that can only grow weaker with age because it is not cultivated. If resources are what we use up, then the one who confuses his source with his resource can only in the end appear depleted.

Note that the discriminator may have a soft as well as a hard face. The soft face of discrimination is the face of one who is charmed by cultural difference, who finds variation of usages an amusing natural display. Such a charming spectacle is produced by regarding cultural difference aesthetically, i.e., as an array of objects that is pleasing in its colour and its unusualness of form.[2] The one who is charmed discriminates between his own culture, which, being mundane and familiar, is not charming, and the cultures of others, which are. The difference between the two is, for the one who is charmed, merely a matter of knowledge. For him, knowing means becoming familiar, a process which exhausts the novelty of what was once charming. Deeply, for the discriminator, knowledge is destructive of charm — knowledge is disenchantment. What is enchanting (charming) is what is (what exists) apart from need. The discriminator needs his own culture, but does not recognize a need for that of others. When he familiarizes himself with the ways of others he sees them as being as much a product of need as his own. He is in no sense influenced by what charms him, he takes it that one ought be influenced only by what is one's own, and what he owns are the usages of his culture. The harsh face of discrimination maintains the same distinction between what is his and what belongs to others, but he is not amused by the other — he seeks to eliminate it. So the soft kind of discrimination may wish to preserve cultural difference while the harsh kind wishes to eliminate it, but the discriminator never cultivates difference, never accepts responsibility for difference, because deeply he takes it as a natural fact.

The one who takes responsibility for difference might be the one who, rather than being charmed or repulsed by difference, is instead inspired by it. To be inspired is to be awakened and animated within oneself, to be no longer controlled by what is outside, rather to recognize, through another, one's own desire. Here, the other serves to open oneself to one's own source. The other is seen as using his resources, the usages with which he is familiar, in a creative way, in a way that permits the other to show that what he needs is an occasion to display his desire. To be inspired is to see the situations of the self and the other as similar inasmuch as what both require is recognition that usage is employed in order to activate desire. To be inspired is to feel one's own desire as the source of one's use of resources, and hence no longer to be controlled by usage — no longer need to preserve usage by merely repeating it. To be inspired by the other is to see the other as an example and not as what it to control or be controlled.

The multiculturalist is thus one who needs cultural difference as the source of the examples from which he draws his own life. He is not concerned to insulate himself from the other, for he sees that to do so is to decrease his vitality, not to protect it. For him, life is not to be protected — it is to be cultivated. His aim is to continuously produce more inspiring examples, rather than to contemplate previous ones. He sees that what others take to be his possessions (the usages with which he is familiar) are only useful to his life if they are taken as examples of the desire for the good; if they are taken as good then there is no longer a reason to live but only an uninspired repetition of life's habits.

## Multiculturalism and Canadian Nationalism

Let us consider Canada. What is it? To many it is a familiar matter — Canada is our country and we are Canadians. Often the meaning of such assertions is uncertain, and a frequent strategy for inducing certainty (i.e., for limiting what can be asserted) is to conceive of Canada as other to or different from its milieu of other countries, e.g., the United States and Britain, but a similar contrast could be produced between Canada and any other country. This version of Canada is not very helpful to one seeking to be a Canadian, e.g., an immigrant, or to one seeking to be a better Canadian, or to make Canada better — for while it says Canada is different from others, it leaves quite unsaid what Canada *is*, and overlooks the particularly Canadian way of responding to that question. This is not, then, our approach.

For us, a country is a community gathered on land. As such, a country seems to have two fundamental aspects — one analytic and one concrete. The community is the analytic aspect of a country; a community is a social entity which is, strictly speaking, ideal — visible in itself but visible in its traces, signs, and representations. For us, a country is a community that gathers and limits itself by relating itself to its own representations in such a way that these relations are recognized as the practical rule of life for that community. These relations are sovereign — which is not to say exclusive or singular — rather, more powerful, more inviting than others. A country is a community that limits itself decisively by respecting a representation of itself as sovereign. A community becomes visible to itself through its representations, which is to suggest that until we see ourselves for a second time (as re-presented), we do not see ourselves at all. To simply be present one to another (e.g., as in a crowd on a city street), is not to be present as a community. A community exists as a particular milieu of representations. These are communal usages — without which there can be no community. The community that not only relates itself to itself, but decisively prefers these representations within a geographic terrain, is a country.

Now we can see how a country could be thought of concretely as a familiar landscape — a landscape made familiar by being organized by a sovereign rule. We understand the idea of soil or native land as a metaphor for a milieu of action, i.e., a representation of the community itself. The land is an apt metaphor; its aptness is its deceptiveness — it is easy to forget that when one speaks of one's native soil one does not speak of the wild soil, that one is not speaking literally, but of the soil cultivated by one's own and one's ancestors' sweat, tears, and blood. Deeply, the land or soil upon which a community is gathered is constituted as the representation or usages of the community.

Consider another metaphor that seems to operate in a similar manner: race. The idea of a racial community is the idea of a community with no need for representation. The racial community is the idea of a community of unmediated presence. Since all representations and signs are instances of mediation (instances of what is social and cultural), the racial ideal is grounded in the body, in what is treated as prior to culture — in blood, it is said. The metaphoric character of race, however, is revealed in the practice of organizing a racial community. Such practical organizational work can only be undertaken on the basis of something other than race, namely: usages, such as discriminable racial features (e.g., skin colour, body type, facial or cranial features, and the like), or presumptive indices thereof (e.g., geneological lineage, institutional affiliation, and the like). So in the organizational practice of racial identification, reference is necessarily made to race-as-representation-of-race, and the racial community is revealed as quite other to its ideal of unity as unmediated co-presence.

We can now see that two of the concrete versions of the possibility of a country — common native soil and common racial constitution — are themselves instances of the very practice of representation that their use seeks to overcome. We take it that this practice of collective representation, fundamental to the existence of a country, is the practice of the creation and enactment of culture.

The one who loves and exclusively prefers his or her country, and conceives it in terms of race or soil, is understood as a nationalist — the nation is the people, conceived as a racial (natural, biological) community, united with its native (natural soil) and represented as a cultural entity. The nationalist is the actor whose conduct is controlled by the desire to be one with his milieu and the need to make the milieu worthy of such intimacy. His concern is to practice representation concretely, i.e., to use representations discriminately rather than in an inspired way. His interest is to preserve the purity of the milieu and of the nation rather than to use them in a way that would reveal what such usage represents. The life of the nationalist is centred in his country *as if the country were what is represented* rather than recognizing the *the country is a style or practice of representation.* The nationalist treats his country as if it were a nation, and his nation as if it were a thing. In contrast, the multiculturalist is controlled by at least two centres, and his conduct continuously draws its inspiration (represents itself) from the difference and tension of the two. The multiculturalist is elliptical, the nationalist is circular. If the circle is an image of centred clarity, the ellipse, because it has more than one focus, is unclear — a blur or mosaic, a collage.

The frequently lamented Canadian uncertainty and irresolution with respect to its identity is thus not necessarily a weakness or problem to be overcome. It would only be so from the perspective of one who preferred clarity. Clarity is not a prerequisite of solidarity; rather, it is merely a particular form of solidarity. It is not the Canadian form. This is what the nationalist frequently laments. The Canadian form of solidarity *in fact* is the form de-centrism. Canada has two major cultural centres — English and French. Every effort to deny this fact (to produce a single centre) results in a reaffirmation of it. Canada's form of solidarity is dispersion. Even English Canada, which most conceives itself as *the* centre, finds that its own centre (Toronto) cannot hold — for the West of Canada contests Toronto's claim to represent Anglophone Canada, while the postwar vitality and growth of Toronto itself has in the main been provided for by the creation, through immigration, of large communities of non-English origin. Just as much, English attempts to control Québec have resulted in a renaissance of action grounded in a denial of the English version of Canada and an affirmation of Québec as a country.

The Canadian weakness is the inappropriateness of its relation to its representations. The Canadian weakness is its non-recognition of its strength. The Canadian problem is that it has been dominated by the naïve assumption that solidarity requires a strong and singular centre — it does not see the possibility that a strong solidarity can result from a plurality of eccentric foci. The historically dominant English-Canadian habit is to repress the existence of centres other than itself, and to be offended if it encounters the representations of another centre.[3] The English habit is to think only one centre is possible for it, and so it seeks to insulate itself from influence by the representations of others. These practices are inappropriate to Canada, however appropriate they may be to an insular people.

## Some Examples

Let us consider three quotidian, yet revealing, examples of insular practices, and one example of an eccentric alternative. The first example is provided by the appearance in English of René Lévesque's *La Passion du Québec*. The title of the work appears in translation as *My Québec*, as opposed to the literal translation: "The Passion of Québec." Our interest is to understand the sense of the difference between "My Québec" and "The Passion of Québec."

We note immediately that the specific rule of mistranslation exemplified in this construction involves two moves: (a) substitution (of "My" for "La Passion du") and (b) relocation (of "La Passion du" in the interior of the book).[4] Hence the rule does not enact the substitution in every instance of passion, but apparently only in cases involving a public or civil order, i.e., the rule requires the segregation of passion and public order. Here we perhaps have an instance covered by the same principle as that which organizes the belief that "the state has no place in the bedrooms of the nation." But the state is clearly concerned to both take its place in the nation's façades — its public representations — and to conceal its place in creating the very difference between interior and exterior which it then defends as natural.

The principle governing the English translation forbids the appearance of passion in the order of the text's title. The title is the public face of the text — that which appears in bibliographic lists and arrays on bookstore shelves and in homes. The rule forbidding the appearance of passion is not the exclusive possession of the English, for it is a feature of many worlds: the world of etiquette, the world of the state, of diplomacy and correctness of form. Such too is the world of grammar as a concern for the proprieties of language. But these proprieties are ordered differently in different worlds. Hence the mistranslation sacrifices the rules of grammar in order to preserve the rule of insular culture. The world of propriety cannot eliminate passion, but it does transform and relocate it; strictly speaking, then, it represses it.

Note also that the substitution employed personalizes the text, makes it a matter of someone's property, and suggests a private individual's point of view. It denies that the author seeks to speak on behalf of, or as a representative of, a particular constituency or community — a community identified in French by reference to its passion. For the work to appear in the English world, it must become the property of a private person; it must be deprived of its cultural context and appear as contextless. But the private property of the passionless individual is *not* an example of *lack* of context, it is an example of the milieu of English Canada, the milieu of the passionate insularity of capitalism, individualism, and private property. For Lévesque to appear in English Canada, he must appear as already like the English; he must not suggest his specific difference — that he is grounded in a milieu of collective passion rather than individual property. Hence his context is rendered invisible by substituting a foreign context, which by virtue of its familiarity to the English reader, is also invisible, i.e., overlooked.

The enactment of these particular practices of culturally repressive propriety is an instance of the denial or non-enactment of multiculturalism. It is a denial that is particularly ironic in terms of the context of its enactment: a text which speaks of the very matter which the repression enacts. The very speech which details and is grounded in a history of Québec's suffering centuries of English mutilation undergoes still another wounding in order to cry out. The cry itself is mutilated — Lévesque as writer is systematically and doubly deformed by his life of humiliation. He tries to be free through writing, but the writing itself suffers the same fate as both that which it writes for, and the one who writes it.[5]

The conclusion that we draw from this example concerns the character of the difference between the multicultural impulse and the cultural impulse. Multiculturalism is not a natural possibility for an insular (cultural) actor. It is what one would call a rational, conscious, or artful possibility. As such, it is constantly subverted by the natural impulses of its own supporters.

The 1979 annual report of the Ontario Advisory Council on Multiculturalism as reported in the *Toronto Star* of August 11, 1979, aptly illustrates this tragedy and provides our second example. The report concerns "the indifference and lack of involvement [of the Ontario press] in the interests and problems of ethnocultural groups." Here, a concept, "ethnocultural," is generated by those who seek to speak for multiculturalism, but it is a concept and a speaking that is blind to its own centre. By failing to see both the Ontario press *and itself* as representative of English-Canadian culture, the report fails to see insularity as a cultural feature of English-Canadian life. Its blindness is its creation of a linguistic monstrosity — a self-doubling blur — in order to avoid treating English-Canadian culture as "ethnic," i.e., as a particular and limited way of life. This insular life — a life disinterested in the lives of others — is the same life that reproduces itself by producing notions like "ethnocultural." The ethnocultural is meant to be all that the English are not, and by thinking so the English need never confront their own ethnicity. Hence we see the sterility of insularity as its habit of re-producing itself rather than producing a lively other.

A third concrete example was provided during CBC coverage of the 1979 Federal election, when a sign of deep difference ("dualism") was perceived as "profoundly disturbing" and "horrifying" by a distinguished representative of English-Canadian cultural national-ism, Pierre Berton, in the context of commenting on the political division between French (Liberal) and English (Conservative) voters.

We take it that what is disturbing to the insular nationalist is that the nation is shown to be divided into two cultural constituencies or centres, and that no party can speak for the whole. The whole will have no voice, the whole is silent, and the silence of desire is disturbing. The insular attitude represses the voice of desire and is disturbed by the ensuing silence that we hear as the muted and mutilated voice of its own desire. The insular one wishes to be undisturbed. If the silent voice of desire is disturbing, what would be consoling would be for a part (any part, any party) to speak on behalf of the whole such that the partial speech could adequately represent the whole. When any party speaks, Berton can only hear it as voicing its desire, i.e., its partiality and its sense of needing and wanting. All appear as dissatisfied for none can claim the whole. The insular ideal (its desire) would be a circumstance wherein an authoritative, full, and rich voice could be heard such that the voice of need (e.g., a minority party) would not have to be attended to. Such a full voice implies a full programme of daily business for the citizen; it would employ his energy, provide for his needs, and satisfy his desires.[6] These are, for insularity, desired features of a good life — deep grammatical expectations against which speakers are judged.

Berton cannot desire a speaker whose speaking would reveal a wound, whose speech would be less than full, because such a speaker is an affront to the requirement of etiquette that good speakers appear as lacking nothing, as correct and clean in form, as beautiful. If a speech is incomplete, broken or twisted, deformed or soiled, it cannot be taken as an adequate example of what is true to the whole. The whole is only conceivable to Berton as complete, flawless, and wholesome. So if a wound exists it ought be covered, its opening closed. Horror is a sign of the desire to preserve unbroken exteriors. The wound or deformity of a community is the sign of its bond with its members. By displaying this mark the bond of elector and representative is validated. Yet the rule of etiquette is that it not be displayed; hence the whole, as what wounds every party, always *remains to be said*, or as Lévesque says, "is to be negotiated."

The rule of etiquette is that need never be shown, because to do so is to bring discomfort to another, to cause him to suffer. The result of the rule is that *all* suffer, but each must deny the good of his suffering — hence none may publicly deploy or acknowledge the sign of his bond with the other. Curiously, the bond displaced by this strategy reappears as the insular separation of individualism. The displaced sign of membership in this community of etiquette reappears *negatively* as each member's insular self-sufficiency.

The insular actor cannot imagine a unity that is not present at hand, its boundary secured by an available charter or agreement or structure. It is such an available and unproblematic image of the whole that he seeks to preserve from hazard. Such a bounty would indeed be consoling to one who could give no deep place to passion, but would place himself as the conservator of what is his own. Berton doesn't see that where no party encompasses the whole (e.g., has a majority, or at least draws support from all divisions) *each* party has an opportunity to speak *of* the whole, by speaking *for* its own version thereof. Hence each party will have to make its version desirable and will reveal that it speaks on behalf of its desire. Berton knows that in such a circumstance he can only hear speech as partisan, as desirous, hence Canada becomes an invisible object of desire which can only be revealed in negotiation between passionately interested speakers. Perhaps the risk here is that each party will confuse its interest (its usage or version of the whole) with that of the whole. The risk is that the speaker will fail to see how he deeply needs the irritating other to remind him of the partiality (the passionate character) of his speech, i.e., the risk is that the several parties would fail to see that they are moved by their need of the whole when they are disturbed.

To the insular way of thinking, one who speaks out of need is weak when what is needed is strength. This perspective has an uninspired vision of strength — a vision that does not treat its version of strength as an example thereof, but rather sees itself as strong and what is other than it as weak. It forgets that its power to endure is measured against the strength of the desire it resists.

As a final and contrasting example let us consider an interesting version of multiculturalism as a concrete, mundane, and eccentric linguistic practice which has attained a sufficient degree of stability (e.g., in certain rural zones of Québec's Eastern Townships) to have received a name — its name is *moitié-à-moitié*, half and half. The practice is that of a kind of bilingualism wherein the speaker alternates between speaking French and English — *without regard for either the meaningful or grammatical order of what is being said or to whom he is speaking.* Hence the speaker operates the usages and grammars of two languages in such a way that unity of expression and sense is artfully generated. Two forms of life are at once strictly preserved *and* shown to be matters of indifference. What makes a difference is the *use* of two languages in such a way as to demonstrate the importance of their *difference* as the resource which is used to express and constitute a form of life unique to and co-temporal with their interaction. It is an elusive and eccentric play which dances on the preserved ruins of two obviously present centres.

*Moitié-à-moitié* reveals an actor who is rooted in two grounds at once, and who sees this dual origin as precious and necessary to herself. Each is sovereign within its domain of usage and each domain yields to the other without regret or resistance, knowing that the other will shortly do the same to it. Hence their association is silently present all the while that either speaks. To the insular ear the conversations thereby produced have an unsettlingly prefatory character; it is as if one is continuously waiting for the speaker(s) to lapse into their native tongue, not realizing that each speaker *is* speaking her native tongue. Concretely, their parents may themselves each have been raised in a bilingual home and community.

Could this be a version of how a native Canadian speaks? An example of practical multi-cultural life as distinct from Multiculturalism as an abstract ideology or government programme? This suggestion is grounded in an understanding of culture as a mundane and daily practice characterized by its ordinariness and unremarkability. Culture is a limit of life which all members respect by employing its usages naturally, hence centring their conduct in the field constituted by the community of users. In the case of *moitié-à-moitié* the field is constituted, either historically or presently, by need and desire — historically in the degree that the union of man and woman as father and mother is an accomplishment of both need and desire, and presently in the degree that rural life requires that neighbours both need and desire one another's co-presence as assistance and company. *Moitié-à-moitié* is a practical, i.e., spoken, version of multiculturalism which is analogous to the practice of sovereignty-association. In it each language retains its sovereign integrity, yet the integrity of both its sense and form is only achieved in its use in association with another sovereign form. Each is the supplement to the other in the practical conduct of life.

## Conclusion

To see unity as preferably undifferentiated is a cultural trait, a fundamental element of insularity as a particular form of social life. The form of life understood as multicultural, in contrast, takes it that the strongest form of unity is that which obtains between deeply different elements. Their unity is that of passion — of yearning for that which is other to the natural or given constitution of the elements.

The strength of such a relation — a relation of desire — is different from the strength of insularity. Desire's power is to move and to be moved — desire and passion are the signs or representations of our being (or having been) moved by the other. The strength of insularity, in contrast, is to endure. Insulation is an inhibition of motion; it seeks to preserve and secure its object from influence. For it, influence can only result in dissipation — a wasting of itself — a corrupting of its excellence or wearing away of its distinction. The unity of Canada (its multicultural life) is the unity of desire and endurance, a relation that seems endlessly fated to resurface in different dialogic forms. In its insular form, it becomes visible as the relation of conquered-victor, two solitudes, two scorpions in a bottle. In its eccentric form, it becomes visible as *moitié-à-moitié* — half and half. Each form associates desire and endurance in a distinctive manner. Both seem illustrative of Canadian life as ruled by a multicultural limit.

## Notes

1   Appreciation is acknowledged to Professors Hédi Bouraoui, Michael Lustigman, and Hans Mohr for their critical readings of an earlier version of this text.

2   A concrete example of such a spectacle elevated to the level of a civic festival may be seen in the annual Metropolitan Toronto Caravan.

3   If it sees French on its food containers it gags — it says French is being forced down its throat.

4   Interestingly, the first instance of the reappearance of this material is in the exergue, which is not produced by the author of the text, but by its publisher, the one who in this case is responsible for the mistranslation in the first place. Hence the exergue is physically interior to the book but exterior to the authored text.

5   The same dynamic rules Lévesque's political programme, but this cannot be developed at this time.

6   Recall here Berton's enthusiasm for such programmes in the past — railroad building, gold rushing, and the like.

JAMES N. PORTER received his Ph.D. in Sociology from Duke University in 1972. He has been on the faculty of York University since 1969 and is currently Associate Professor of Sociology and Social and Political Sciences. His intellectual interests are in social theory.

# Relevance of Unity
## to Multiculturalism

### Alex Chumak

It appears to be difficult in October 1979 to talk about both Canadian unity and cultural pluralism, or multiculturalism, especially if the media is screaming about fixed oil prices, high interest rates, foreign policy, and so on. Furthermore, it seems that both unity and multiculturalism have been debated, discussed, and studied in great detail and to the point of exhaustion. However, I should like to approach them from a different perspective — not historical, religious, or sociological — but, in my opinion, realistic and human.

The November 1976 election results in Québec precipitated an unusual interest in our country and its future. Numerous unity groups sprang up around the country. The press carried daily reports on Canada's future. Attempts were being made to answer questions such as "Will Canada survive? Will Québec secede? What will be our future?" and so on.

Perhaps the most significant document to emerge in January of this year, which analyzed the problem and recommended solutions, was the Task Force on Unity, co-chaired by John Robarts and Jean-Luc Pepin. An impressive study, it dealt with every topic ranging from the role of the monarchy to the individual and collective rights, but unfortunately it minimized the role of the ethnic groups.

An immediate question occurs, before I go on — Where is the

report today? Are its recommendations being implemented? If so, why do we not know or hear about it?

The second issue, of cultural plurality or multiculturalism, has also been thoroughly discussed and debated.

Since the Commission on Bilingualism and Biculturalism in the early 1960s, ethnic groups all over Canada tried to have some input towards establishing a multicultural policy for the country. Concepts such as multiculturalism, one nation — many cultures, bilingual — multicultural, etc., began to surface.

However, after all this time, it is my contention that there is still no established and firm policy within the federal government and provincial governments, to spell out clearly and concisely what the multicultural policy is.

Prior to writing this paper, I called both the federal and provincial governments to try to find out verbally what the respective policy of each level is. Neither spokesman could adequately explain multiculturalism apart from platitudes and pleasant sounding words and phrases.

Thus, we find ourselves in the situation where Canadian unity is threatened while the culturally pluralistic groups on one side of the coin are saying, "We should be involved," but on the other side are not fully aware of themselves and their places in the Canadian mosaic. Hence, the dilemma, is there, or should there be any relation between the cultural groups and national unity, or put in another way, should the ethno-cultural groups be concerned about the future of Canada, vis-à-vis the status of Québec?

Can a group, which represents roughly one-third of the country's population, become legitimately involved in what is reported to be essentially a French-English problem? Or, should we, as multicultural groups, define the problem in our terms, and proceed to join the debate? The latter is preferable to me since, as citizens of the country, we play an integral role, and we have every constitutional right to involve ourselves. We have a vested interest in Canadian unity. Sadly, we have not participated to the extent that we should.

I should like, at this point, to return to what I remarked earlier. What happened to the recommendations in the Robarts-Pepin Report? The report, in my opinion, adequately spelled out the problems of the French and the English, and for those groups proposed what I thought were adequate solutions. But since the completion of the report we have heard little, if anything, about National Unity. Before the 1979 federal election, the Liberal Party of Canada made unity an issue — Where is this Party today? What relevance does unity have today? What priority? What does the present government think about it? It was not even mentioned in the Throne Speech on October 9, 1979.

It almost leads one to believe that unity was an election tactic, used to its fullest, in order to try to obtain as much support as possible from the electorate.

But, I submit, that is wrong. Unity is perhaps one of the most serious problems that this country has ever faced, despite the fact that the press is no longer writing about it. If Québec opts out of Confederation, and thereby destroys Canadian unity, we can, without doubt, kiss multiculturalism (whatever it is, it certainly is something worth pursuing) goodbye. We can forget about our own "special statuses," since it can be argued, and quite rightly, that it was because of Québec that Canada has not adopted the American "melting pot" approach. By giving Québec special consideration and a special status, the federal government by extension could give similar recognition to Ukranians, Germans, Balts, Polish, and so on. That is not to say that each group will get a province of its own, but simply if one group is recognized, then it should follow that others should as well.

For this reason (and there are others — nationalistic, patriotic), Québec must not separate. Put simplistically, if Québec separates, Canada could turn into a melting pot.

What should multicultural groups do, if anything, to preserve the unity of our nation?

There are, in my opinion, many things we can do. Allow me just to elaborate on a few:

In the first place, we, as multicultural Canadians, must get involved in issues and topics other than our immediate parameters. For example, how many of us supported the use of French in the air controllers' debate? How many of us take the time to acquaint ourselves with the history of Canada, and the role played by French Canadians? In other words, how informed are we about Canadian history?

Secondly, we cannot restrict our activities, our ethnic press, and our media to our exclusive multicultural way of life. We, as Canadians, have another dimension — that is, we are Canadians of many unique backgrounds. How many times do we as Canadians of various backgrounds get involved in preparing briefs on matters that do not directly affect us as ethnics? I have in mind trade agreements, economics, international relations, environmental concerns, and so on. We must mature and get involved in these and other matters. If we don't, multiculturalism will only be interpreted as "eating and dancing." Surely we deserve more than that. Surely we have matured to the extent where we can voice our concerns in a competent manner.

Thirdly, we as multicultural groups must stop demanding favours and stop complaining that we are treated unfairly. No one will take pity on us. No one will give us something for nothing. What we must do, on the other hand, is to produce informed, educated, professional individuals who will, because of their professionalism, stand on their own. We are too often placated by a grant to put on a multicultural festival. How often do we hold a symposium, for example, to deal with education, foreign affairs, or, very recently, the International Year of the Child?

How does this tie in with unity? What relevance does multiculturalism have towards unity?

There is no question in my mind that if the French-speaking Canadians would perceive support and understanding from us, the multicultural groups, then they would feel more compelled to join with us, and remain in Canada and Confederation. Further, there is no question in my mind that if we, as ethno-cultural Canadians, obtain sound and accurate knowledge about Canadian history and Canadian issues, we would be more readily accepted and respected.

If the Anglo-Celtics are aware that we are getting involved in Canadian issues, we can expect a change in their attitude, and most likely a completely different approach towards multiculturalism. A policy with reality and meaning would be formulated, rather than the "eating and dancing syndrome" that all of us find unacceptable. Through this, we would become more united and find much more in common, than we have today. We would have common goals in a common country.

Lastly, through our accomplishments and achievements in business, education, science, etc., and I may add, by running for political office at all levels, we demonstrate to both the francophones and the Anglo-Celtics that we are equal to them, and just as competent. We will be invited to participate in the real issues of this country.

In summary, I should like to state that despite the fact that the press and media are no longer talking about unity, we must. Despite the fact that it appears to be a non-issue, we must make it an issue. We must demonstrate to Canada that we care, since Canada is currently faced with its greatest crisis since 1867.

"We yawn while the country crumbles."


ALEX CHUMAK received a B.A. in Sociology and Psychology at the University of Ottawa in 1967 and an M.A. in Applied Criminology in 1974. He is a part-time lecturer at the Ryerson Polytechnical Institute, Faculty of Social Sciences, Social Work Department. As Trustee to the Toronto Board of Education, Ward 1, he served in the following capacities: Chairman of the Race Relations and Multiculturalism, of the Third Languages Committee, and of the Guidance and Counselling Committee. In 1979, he has planned and co-chaired a Symposium, *Ontario Outlook '79*, which examined the viewpoints of cultural minorities towards a renewed Confederation.

# The Individual
# in a Multicultural Society

Jamshed Mavalwala

Canada can pride itself not only on being a country that presents a physical variety from coast to coast and north to south that is matched by few other nations, but also Canada can truly pride itself on a diversity that is far richer: the exciting cultural diversity of its people. In our relatively small population of over twenty-two million people, we possess the cultures of nearly all the far-flung corners of the globe.

Our contemporary Canadian society is made up of a truly bewildering diversity of cultures and their concomitant languages and customs. While other societies divide their individuals into socio-economic groups, we have another distinction that we have deliberately chosen to contend with. We call it ethnicity. The roles that individuals play in Canadian society are determined by many sets of parameters and we must examine them with care and come to an understanding of them if we are to understand how best we, as individuals, can function in contemporary Canadian society.

Historically, we have a sad record of cruelty towards the native people and today that legacy of mistrust still lingers. As European communities settled in Canada, they did not settle as equals, and communities such as the Ukranian people paid a high price before being accepted as citizens in Canada. It was not unusual for people of German or Dutch descent to warn their children to speak their native tongue *only* in the home for fear of public ridicule. Some of Canada's ugliest times were the bigotry and hatred shown in the first decades of this century towards the Chinese communities of British Columbia. The smaller Japanese and Sikh immigrant communities also were harshly treated on the West Coast.

As we come to understand that we of the human race are truly on one planet passing together through space, our relationships to each other have been modified. Radio, telegraph, film, and now television keep us instantly and, often painfully, accurately informed of what we do to each other.

All this has caused us to look closely at other Canadians and realize that no one culture or way of life has ever been superior to any other, and that it is possible for us to live together in harmony and survive collectively to create a better neighbourhood, city, province, and thereby country. This changing attitude of Canadians, tired of bigotry and prejudice, was accurately reflected in the policy of Multiculturalism that was presented before Parliament in November 1971 by the then Prime Minister of Canada, Pierre Elliott Trudeau. The policy that was unanimously accepted by Parliament clearly stated that the government would assist *all* Canadian cultural groups to develop in Canada, and to achieve *full* participation in Canadian society. Multiculturalism can best be seen as an ethic that should pervade our lives at all times, wherein we see each and every individual within his or her own context.

I see multiculturalism as a basic ethic that says that each person is an individual in her or his own right and has the right to be treated as such. Under this view of multiculturalism our society should be permeated with this ethic in all its aspects and at all times. Thus we understand that multiculturalism is not a program handed to us, or a course to take in a classroom but an integral part of each and every one of us. The philosophy of multi-culturalism says that individuals should be able to choose their own identity and to freely live with this identity so long as they do not impinge on the rights of others.

Consider for a moment what multiculturalism is not. It is not people living under the mantle of ethnicity. It is in a multi-ethnic society that we divide human beings into ethnic groups, and then deliberately choose to deal with them in that context. That is definitely not our goal in Canada. We do not wish to divide Canadians under ethnic labels, often inaccurately given and often grossly misinterpreted. No individual lives in Canada *only* to indulge in "ethnic food" and "ethnic dance." These activities are only a part of the life of individuals whose major concern is to create a better world for themselves and the generations to come. Myriad factors go into making up an individual's identity and often ethnicity plays a minor role. In a multicultural society it is individuals who choose how much ethnicity to incorporate into their lives. In an ethnicity-based society this is externally imposed.

The major advantage of a multicultural society is that in accepting the basic philosophy of multiculturalism, we postulate a society that listens to, and accepts, the identity that is being projected by each individual. We are far more likely to come to a better understanding of a society if we listen to what its members have to say about themselves than if we arbitrarily decide their identity.

This philosophy sounds simple and it is easy for us to say that we are a multicultural society. But in fact we are still only on the road towards this goal. At present we are a nation of many ethnic groups striving to preserve our own identities and then project these identities to others. Some groups are further along the road than others. Our goal is a society where the culture of one's own upbringing will be accepted naturally by all, and where each of us can preserve the heritage of our own choice, freely, so long as we do not impose on the rights of others. This is not an idle dream of the future, for the realization can be seen in many parts of Canada today.

In following the road towards the goal of a multicultural society we must avoid being trapped on the wayside by ethnicity. What we do not want is a plethora of ethnic communities each with its own section of society, but rather a true participation in all levels of society by all types of people.

One misconception that many of us harbour is that such a change in society can only be brought about by group action, the ultimate group being "the government." Ten years of observing change in Canada have led me to believe that here as elsewhere there is a big role to be played by the individual. There are, of course, many types of actions that are best taken by groups ranging from neighbourhood groups such as ratepayers associations to national groups of millions of people, but in that process let us not forget the role that you, and everyone else, as individuals, can and must play.

How can we as individuals, living in a complex society, further the philosophy of multiculturalism and help achieve a society that will be uniquely Canadian? The process that I propose is simple but its execution demands both perseverance and patience.

## The Process

There are three major phases towards achieving a multicultural society:

### Phase One
I can only understand the behaviour of others if I understand myself. Therefore I must look at myself and learn why I do things the way I do, within the context of my own culture. When I have begun to understand the way my own culture affects me then...

### Phase Two
...I can begin to try to understand other individuals from other cultures. I will do this in the same way as Phase One, with patience, for I now realize the complexity of interactions taking place between an individual and his or her own cultural envelope.

### Phase Three
I will resist the temptation to go to either extreme. I will not belittle other ways of life and I will not denigrate my own way of life. I will strive for the balance of a multicultural person who has learned to accept his own cultural identity with all its logic and its inconsistencies, and to see others as they would prefer to be seen. Acquiring such a balance is not easy and will require constant alertness.

Let us spend a few moments examining how to proceed with Phase One. Our greatest hurdle in understanding ourselves in the context of our own cultural envelopes is that we do not realize just how enormously our culture influences our lives. Just stop and think for a moment how much influence is brought to bear upon us from the moment we are conceived. From our earliest moments of consciousness our own culture tells us how to act, and react, when to laugh, when to cry, when to do neither and withhold emotion. Our first hurdle is to recognize that there is *no* free society. All societies impose codes of conduct that demand to be followed. We think we make logical, intelligent decisions in our lives, that we make and direct our culture according to logical and sensible rules. We have to learn to recognize the fact that our culture, like all others, is a growth of millions of factors, has grown over many, many years, and is in a state of constant change.

Let us look at a few examples. Our culture not only tells us whom we should marry but also directs us as to how and when we will fall in love, and how to behave when we are in that state. We will quickly recognize how many changes have taken place. Only a few years ago "Mr. Right" was the movie star image of a successful (in terms of money) man, clean shaven, young, driving a car (preferably a convertible), and a long list of other attributes that I am sure will come to your mind. "Miss Right" had a clear complexion, had, or aspired to after hours of sometimes painful manipulation, naturally curly hair, smelled of the current fashion of perfume, spoke softly, danced well, and was bright but not too bright. Agreed, short, fat, and pimply people also did fall in love and sometimes found this emotion returned. But the general trend was to expect those among us who did not fit our concepts of beauty to spend a long time propped up against the gym wall during school dances.

It is possible as we approach 1980 to remember a time when being thin was considered tantamount to having tuberculosis. Many thousands of thin people grew up in this country being pinched on the upper arm by caring, and therefore interfering, relatives and being constantly cajoled to "eat, eat." Now only a few years later what was a healthy plump girl who would obviously make someone a good wife is seen as somewhat overweight and the same skinny physique that evoked expressions of concern is now admired as a "lovely" figure. In other words we went from a "plump" concept of beauty to a practically emaciated "thin" concept of beauty. Love was an emotion to be felt for a person who possessed the correct quantities of material possessions. Our culture is riddled with references of the woes that befall those that fall in love with the pauper rather than the prince.

Eating and drinking are other areas that we can use as an example. Even the timing of the evacuation of the bowels is culturally taught. Remember being snatched out of your warm crib and unceremoniously deposited on a cold potty? It had nothing to do with biology. The culture determined the timing. What we eat is culturally determined. We eat parts of certain plants and throw away other parts that are edible. Our ways of food preparation sometimes enhance the food and sometimes destroy its nutritive value. A good example of how illogical we are with food is the way in which we process our staple food, bread, so that it will be "white" and "refined," and then spend more time and money adding back those very ingredients that had been removed earlier. If you have any doubt about how rigidly your culture determines your eating, try going into a major restaurant in the late evening and ordering porridge, bacon and eggs, toast and coffee. You may only raise eyebrows if you are a valued customer or a local tycoon, but the chances are that even though the kitchen is perfectly capable of providing your request, it is too deviant from the cultural norm to be granted. Conversely think about how difficult it would be to get a steak, rare and juicy, a tossed salad, and a glass of dry red wine at eight o'clock in the morning. Nutritionists know full well that what is good for the body is often flatly rejected by the soul.

Another aspect of our culture is the way our world is molded by the language we speak. People tend to think of their own language as complete and expressive. But we usually use a language in severely limited ways. Both the limits of English and its current usage are well illustrated by the word "love." Just stop and think for a moment about what it must sound like to others when we say "I love God" and "I love my car." Think of what it sounds like to others when they hear people talk of "loving" their wives and also using the same verb to connote feeling towards the family pet. We know what we mean by the word "love" in its varied uses: spiritual (I love God), sexual (I love my spouse), affectionate (I love my child), acquistitive (I love money), emotional (I love music). But do others know exactly what we mean?

Then consider the differences between our ideals and our realities. We constantly remind ourselves of how civilized we are. But we possess better laws to prevent cruelty to dogs than we do to prevent cruelty to children. Anyone who has spent any time at all in helping to alleviate the cruelty that is inflicted on the "battered child" cannot but agree. We say that we love children but consider the many ways in which they are non-persons within this culture. The same culture that boasts its concern over women's liberation also glorifies James Bond. In a country that deals with black skin colour as a "minority problem," millions of dollars are drained out of this country by those who do not possess a dark enough skin and so go south to acquire a tan.

These examples are presented to help us step outside ourselves and realize that others see us very differently. If you have laughed at yourself then you have begun to see yourself with some understanding and some compassion. Our goal is just to recognize that we *are* influenced by our culture. Don't get trapped into judgements. The "good" or "bad" can change. We have learned, again and again, that what was "good" may not have been so good after all and what was "bad" is now seen in a different light.

So our Phase One is to realize, firstly, the pervasiveness and the persuasion of our own cultural envelopes, and secondly, that culture is dynamic and not static and in fact is constantly undergoing revisions.

Having understood how complex our relationships are between ourselves and our own culture, how can we possibly ever hope to learn about anyone else? Here are some individual strategies to use in Phase Two.

We can best approach others by listening to what the individual is saying. How often have we seen a person and allowed the stereotype already fixed in our own mind to speak louder than the real person? We see a "Chinese" face and expect a "Chinese" person. Why do we do this when we also know that this person may have been born and bred in Don Mills, Ontario? We can best avoid stereotypes by constantly questioning value judgements. Once you stop and think about stereotypes you will see how commonly we use them. We have stereotypes about the professions: doctors, nurses, lawyers, politicians, airline stewardesses, garage mechanics, secondhand car salesmen, insurance agents, etc. And yet even when each and everyone of us know that we have personal knowledge of the spurious nature of stereotypes, we still continue to use them. What is worse is when we allow a gross stereotype to pass in converstaion without challenging the speaker.

As you learn to avoid stereotypes and begin to listen to each individual you will quickly realize that these cross-cultural differences which you started out thinking were many, are actually completely overshadowed by similarities. You will also quickly learn that you can only understand another person by giving them the same respect and attention you want yourself. Can you imagine trying to distill the complexity of what it means to be a Canadian into a short diatribe? But how many times have you accepted the banal opinions of others on "the English," or "the French," or "the Greeks," or "the Ukranians?"

In Phase Two it quickly becomes clear that individuals in Canada determine their identity by their socio-economic level, their age, their sex, their religious tradition, and among many other factors, their ethnicity. Try to remember that what you are hearing from other individuals is more important than all the travelogues you have read or all the "instant experts" who, having spent seven days in one hotel in a country, are now confidently telling you all you wish to know about the whole country. Somehow the combination of jet lag and the stupor brought on by too much alcohol and/or too much sun seems to restrain the embarrassment people should show when they blithely speak of *all* of Great Britain, or *all* of the Caribbean after their brief and essentially superficial experience.

Having opened our ears and eyes to other individuals brings us to our final phase, Phase Three. A truly multicultural society does not either reject other cultures or denigrate one's own culture. A good balance is achieved with accepting one's self and accepting others naturally, as individuals first and whatever else second. To live together is also to make sure that one person's rights do not trample upon the rights of others. Those aspects of our cultures that teach us to divide the world must be re-examined very critically. Identifying what is really happening around us and using this reality to help us deal with our own world is not easy. But constant practice soon gives us the ability to look past the masks that individuals wear and gives us the ability to see communities as they really are, not as we imagine them to be.

In our concern to understand ourselves better and to be better understood by others, here are some of the pitfalls we need to learn to avoid.

### 1. Us/Them Dichotomy

We should not encourage solidarity inside a group by making the "Canadian" into the bogey-man. How often do we hear phrases such as "We have to get ourselves together or Canadians will never understand us" as if there is such a thing as a homogeneous Canadian matrix out there. It is particularly easy in the area of race relations to put the blame on "Canadians" or "whites" or a series of other labels. Such negative reinforcement enhances polarization and does nothing to further understanding and reduce anxiety levels. What we need to remember constantly is that we do not use the "outside" groups to generate fear that will force the inside group to solidify. It is possible to enhance a good self-image positively. Positive attitudes will greatly reduce the fear of interacting with others and make the projection of an external identity so much easier.

## 2. One Size Does Not Fit All

We may seek solutions that function superbly to resolve a particular issue. But this same solution does not necessarily promise us the same success if used to resolve the same issue but in another context. For example, a face-to-face discussion session may work very effectively between Person A and Person B but could result in worsening the situation between Persons C and D, because in the latter case there is a considerable amount of work to be done before a face-to-face discussion would work. Charity can become condescension and toleration can become unwilling acceptance, depending on the persons concerned. The best strategies for relations between us are ones that are specifically tailor-made. We need to remain dynamic and not become static in our dealings with others.

## 3. Age Sets, Sex Sets, and Time

Solutions generated to resolve issues need constant re-evaluation and also need to be tested for the different needs of individuals. In some cases, the needs can be different for men and for women and in some cases the resolutions that are acceptable by the adults of a community may be totally unacceptable to the children. What we expect of society today may radically change in the 1980s and yesterday's solutions may be clearly inadequate. Just because a strategy has worked in the past does not necessarily mean that it will prove effective again.

## 4. Feedback Systems

Every time a change is brought about in our complex society, it sets off a chain reaction. Thus, when, in an effort to further understanding between peoples, one particular strategy — the sharing of food and folk dancing — was used, it resulted in bringing together groups in a non-demanding situation. But then a feedback system is set up, and to continue to bring the same two groups together does not advance understanding. It may even lead to resentment. The first step must lead on to the next one or the strategy does not progress.

## 5. Response Reactions

All the agencies and groups function because they are responding to some inequities that they see in society. We need to be careful that all our efforts are not taken up responding to "crisis situations" and that we still have some time and energy left to attack long-term issues. It is relatively easy to become problem-oriented thereby allowing major but non-crisis matters to slide by unattended. Crises must be dealt with but our ultimate goal is to change attitudes, and that only happens slowly over a long period of time.

## 6. Redundancy

As soon as we get together, some redundancy becomes apparent in ideas and programmes. But in actual fact there is no redundancy at all. If one group in Mississauga is doing exactly what another group in Scarborough is doing, that is not redundancy because their target populations are completely separate. At the moment we need much more volunteer effort. There are just simply not enough people to do the work that is necessary to continue to improve relations in our society.

In the final analysis you should see yourself as the responsible fulcrum on which the world in which you live in, rests. While there are areas where individuals are relatively powerless in the short term, just stop and examine the changes in world history that have been brought about by individuals. Who would have thought that a young boy growing up in a carpenter's family in the ancient Middle East would be remembered twenty centuries later? Every culture is the sum total of the behaviour of all its individuals and our universe is reflected in all of us. By underestimating our potential as individuals, we hand over the responsibility to others who may not either be willing, or have the capacity to create the multicultural society that we wish to see come to fruition.

By becoming multicultural, we gradually can become a nation of human beings who can accept, and often delight in our diversity, see the strengths of our variablity, and impart to our children the knowledge that they have a great advantage in being able to live where they will be accepted and judged for themselves only. It has never been tried before and now for the first time in history we in Canada have the exciting possibility of creating a truly multicultural society: a Canada to which you and I can proudly belong. Because none of us is more Canadian than the next person. Because we can live in Canada, not as Hungarians, or Pakistanis, or as Scotsmen, or whatever, but as you and I. Each in his own way, without fear or embarrassment, secure that as we grow together towards our future, our joy will be when our children turn to each other and wonder what all that fuss about differences was, way back in 1980.

JAMSHED MAVALWALA is chairman of the Council's Education Committee. He received his Ph.D. in Anthropology from Delhi, India, and did post-doctoral work at Harvard. He has taught and researched in Anthropology in India, the United States, Chile, and Canada. Presently on faculty at the University of Toronto, he serves with the Ontario Ministry of Education on the International Development Education Committee of Ontario which advises on and helps to create programmes that will result in better education about developing countries.

# Sociobiology, Prejudice, and Ethnocentrism

Teresa Kott

One of the purposes of this Conference is to examine ways and means in which the intellectual sector of our society can serve the ethnic communities in promoting both the principle and the policy of multiculturalism. It seems to me that the viability of this principle need not to be argued in our gathering. My concern, therefore, is not with its merits but with certain scientific perspectives, concepts, and techniques which may either assist or hinder its implementation.

One such perspective which, if generally accepted, may lead to an escalation of racial and ethnic discrimination, is promoted by sociobiology. This perspective is gaining in popularity among scientists and laymen alike, because of the outstanding discoveries being currently made in the fields of genetics and bioengineering.

Modern sociobiology is no longer anti-environmental. It does acknowledge that evolutionary process in humans involves a complex interplay of genotypical, ecological, and cultural factors. Thus, social relations, social structure, and cultural superstructure are seen as reducible, in the final analysis, to the competition for scarce resources. This competition is universal for all organisms and is aimed at survival of particular gene-clusters. But the way it manifests itself in human relations is no longer thought to be a matter of genetic programming only. In man it is mediated by culture.

Thus, modern sociobiology, though less rigid than in the past, is still reductionist, evolutionist, and materialistic.

If one shares such perspective, one has to assume that the influence of culture notwithstanding, all behaviour is directed at reproductive success. According to the model constructed by a well-known sociobiologist, Pierre van den Berghe, this success can be achieved in three ways: through kin selection, reciprocity, and coercion.

*Kin selection* as a concept rests on the premise that it is imperative for genes to duplicate themselves via reproduction. Since in man and some animals this involves mate-selection, reproduction can best be achieved through cooperation with genetically related organisms. Hence, kin selection is the most important mechanism in ensuring intergenerational transmission of genes.

*Reciprocity* involves organisms' propensity to interact with other organisms for their common benefit, and thus, involves voluntary cooperation. Since its ultimate objective is sexual reproduction, it leads to genetic diversity in the context of kin groups. This propensity, though important in animals, is more so in man because it forms foundations for non-genetically determined behaviour.

*Coercion* may be defined as an ability of an organism to force other organisms to cooperate with it even if such non-voluntary cooperation is detrimental to them. An influential group of social scientists insists that coercion and not reciprocity accounts for all human sociability.

Investigating the implications of the above perspective, one must recognize that it does offer an explanation of the importance of race and ethnicity. In the above terms, race and ethnicity are extensions of kinship, differentiated on phenotypic criteria, and thus, most basic in the identity-formation processes.

Further, this approach may be utilized in the study of social relations. For instance, it may serve to predict circumstances for the emergence of racism and its reduction. It can be applied, as well, to paternalistic relations and other kinds of the superordinate/subordinate relations among racial and ethnic groups.

However, this perspective has some disquieting implications. Recent history demonstrates how scientific theories about superiority of one race influenced the public mind and brought about mass-murder of the "racially inferior" people in the 1940s. It is possible, then, that any reductionist theories pertaining to race and ethnicity may prove instrumental in reviving beliefs in the genetically determined ranking of racial and/or ethnic groupings. Although this particular perspective carries no implications of racism, some workers in the field of biology do claim to have scientific proof of the differential evolutionary advancement among races. Since the propensity towards ethnocentrism seems to be inherent in man, and the tendency to confuse differentiation with stratification is common, as well, this differential evolutionary advancement may be understood as indicative of racial superiority or inferiority. In consequence, we have to be on the alert for any theories which purport to explain human behaviour in terms of the biological perspective.

We cannot assess the validity of this perspective without a thorough knowledge of biology. However, we must keep in mind that the so-called "hard facts" of science tend to be invalidated by new evidence uncovered by research. It may well be that in time a new scientific discovery will indicate that not genes but some previously unsuspected factor or factors are determinants of behaviour. We must remember, also, that to be different does not automatically mean to be superior or inferior and that even the definitions of superiority and inferiority are man-made and can be changed. In sum, we must be conversant with what is new in science and be prepared to deal with those who innocently, or otherwise, may use scientific discovery to justify discrimination.

Several examples of how improper understanding of scientific concepts may affect their utilization for practical purposes are relevant in the context of multiculturalism. For instance, all of us, ethnic minorities included, tend to use the term "ethnic" in relation to ethnic minorities only. We tend to forget that ethnicity is common to all, that in our society the members of the dominant group are of English, Scots, or Welsh origin. By applying the term "ethnic" only to the non-Anglo-Celtic, and non-French groups, we therefore accept and promote the connotations of inferiority associated with this term. We are using the "enemy" language to our own detriment.

Further, we tend to accept a belief that discrimination results from prejudice and so we ignore the instances in which the reverse is true. In this way we neglect research into this dimension. We assume also, that prejudice and stereotyping are always harmful to groups and individuals who are their subjects instead of utilizing these concepts for their benefit. Prejudice, as such, is nothing but a pre-judgement which, in turn, gives rise to stereotyping. Because both prejudice and stereotyping are founded on incomplete and sometimes faulty data and involve over-generalisation, they are commonly condemned as scientifically invalid and/or simplistic. They are condemned as well, because in the realm of racial and ethnic relations prejudice is usually linked with ethnocentrism and consequently racial and ethnic stereotypes are mostly negative.

However, prejudice and stereotyping may work as positive mechanisms in the realm of group relations. They provide insights into the nature of the interacting groups and thus serve as guidelines for behaviour. As such they are not only necessary and indispensable in all social activity but, also, are of interest to social scientists.

For instance, there are two main types of stereotyping encountered in the study of social and race-ethnic relations. One is well-established and resists redefinition regardless of the changing context. It is useless to a scientist as a category depicting groups' traits and it is harmful to all concerned because it ignores the evolutionary processes which each and every group undergoes in the course of its existence. The second type, while adhering to the basic structure of perceptions, allows for the situational changes resulting in re-evaluation, and since it is more flexible, can be useful to a student of group relations on many counts. It may give some indications about the changes within the stereotyped group; it may point out changes in attitudes in the stereotyping group; and it may offer evidence of the change in the relations between the groups in question. Thus, the study of racial and ethnic stereotypes may provide knowledge about racial and ethnic groups. This knowledge in turn may be utilized in redefining stereotypes from negative into positive, or vice versa.

It should be remembered that prejudice and stereotyping are not always negative. One can be prejudiced in favour of an individual or a group. A stereotype of a group can be positive. As we all know, the dominant group is constantly engaged in projecting its own flattering image, and there is no reason why the technique it uses could not be successfully employed by those who want to change the negative images of minorities.

The issue of assimilation is also a subject of many misconceptions. It is frequently argued that the growth of homogenisation in technologically advanced societies threatens the survival of racial and ethnic groups. And the conclusion is: why fight the inevitable? However, there is some evidence that such is not the case. There are indications that homogenisation does not erase the basic attributes of the groups in question because these are rooted in the fundamental values which differentiate one group from another and persist even in the post-industrial type of society.

Furthermore, a popular belief shared by many social scientists holds that assimilation is beneficial to racial and ethnic minorities because the individuals who renounce their racial or ethnic heritage are granted equal status and thus are not hindered in upward mobility. This belief does not account, however, for the instances in which an accultured minority is denied assimilation. Having given up its own cultural identity and group support, it is left then in a void, and becomes alienated from society (Taylor, 1979).

Those in favour of assimilation overlook, as well, the psychological importance of "roots." Again, there is a considerable body of evidence, which suggests that a sense of belonging to a racial or ethnic group possessing its own distinct culture is a necessary factor in personality formation process. The psychologists who support this view maintain that people deprived of such consciousness of kind never reach their full developmental potential. The resulting loss in terms of human resources thus affects not only the individuals who are subjects of such deprivation but also society as a whole (Dabrowski, 1977).

Finally, some comment about the difficulties inherent in the planning of strategies and tactics which may advance multiculturalism seems in order. The example which comes to mind is the Bakke case and its ramifications. This case, famous in the United States and outside of its borders, concerned a white student who was refused admission to a California medical school because of its quota system favouring certain racial and ethnic minorities. Bakke took the school to court, claiming discrimination on the grounds of race, and won on appeal heard by the Federal Supreme Court. However, the verdict rested on an ambiguous decision: the judges agreed that Bakke was discriminated against and must be admitted as a student. But they also agreed that race can be taken into account in admission to the post-secondary educational institutions. What is more, there was a split among the judges as to the legal grounds on which the decision was based. The case itself, and the verdict in question, demonstrate how the laws which protect the interests of racial and ethnic minority groups might be at times at odds with these ensuring the interests of persons.

In societies such as ours the principle of equality for all, regardless of race and ethnicity, may clash at times with the no-less-valued principle of individual rights. The issue, thus, is whether group rights can take precedence over the rights of a person. Public opinion is polarized on the subject and there is no clear-cut solution. Some maintain that the compensatory justice system which imposes racial and ethnic quotas and preferential treatment programmes should be mandatory in all educational and employment situations, in both public and private sectors of society. Others are violently opposed to this, pointing out that such a system would infringe not only on individual rights but also on group rights of the very minorities concerned.

The majority on both sides agree, however, that some compromise must be reached in the interest of social harmony.

One such compromise experimented with in several countries enforces the said quota system and preferential treatment programmes in all institutions and enterprises receiving federal funds or subsidized by the state.

Another formula for a compromise suggests that race and ethnicity should be taken into consideration in admission and hiring policies as a criterion but not as the sole criterion. The proponents of this view argue that since the state should be above favouritism, all state-owned and state-operated agencies, institutions, and enterprises should adhere to the "colour-blind" admission and employment practices based on the merit principle; that the private sector should be left free to act according to the preferential treatment principle; that in the field of higher education, admission and academic performance criteria should be universal for all, regardless of their racial or ethnic background, and that remedial programmes and financial help which will enable the members of racial and ethnic minorities to qualify on merit should be made available to them as a right and not as a privilege (Glazer, 1979).

Still another attempt at constructing a workable compromise borrows from the two models just described, but also adds some elements lacking in both. It proposes that preferential treatment policies in admission and hiring should be binding in all state-owned, state-operated, and state-subsidized agencies and enterprises. The justification here is that only a government has enough power to enforce desegregation and the said policies in the realm of public domain. What is more, the state should assist the private sector in promoting these policies by providing financial and other kinds of incentives in that domain. But it should also offer such support to public and private racially and ethnically closed institutions, agencies, and enterprises, serving the special needs of the particular racial and ethnic groups. Further: preferential treatment in admission and employment practices should not mean that a poorly qualified individual would take precedence over a better qualified one because of his race or ethnicity. What it should mean is an unqualified access to the remedial programmes, tutoring help, and financial aid for members of the minorities in question, which will enable them to compete in academic and employment areas on an equal basis. Thus, according to this third model of compromise, race and ethnicity should be the criteria in the public sector and a criterion in the private sector. Preferential treatment systems should consist of services listed just now, and the access to them should be a right and not a privilege. In the final analysis, personal merit should be the universal criterion in the context of education and employment involving public funds because such an interpretation of the principle of equality seems most likely to promote social harmony.

None of the above models is perfect. However, each of them has some merits. It seems to me, that a forum like this one should devote some of the time at its disposal to examine thoroughly their merits and faults. Such discussion may bring some new insights and ideas about how to solve the issue which, doubtless, is more and more pressing.

Such a discussion on this issue and on the issues upon which I have touched in the preceding parts of this presentation should not end here. It seems to me that it should be taken up in the policy-making sectors of racial and ethnic communities. As previously mentioned, this Conference has as its aim to establish how an institution of higher learning can assist racial and ethnic communities in reaching their goals within the context of the policy of multiculturalism. Scientists, and especially social scientists, can offer facts they discover and theories they build. Racial and ethnic communities can profit through learning about these discoveries and their implications. Conversely, social scientists can learn directly from these communities about problems which are not readily identifiable to any one but an insider.

Since I am a member of an ethnic minority which only now is overcoming the effects of its low entrance status into this society, and since I have some experience with its organizational structure, many such problems are quite familiar to me. This is why I strongly urge this gathering to take up the initiative of the organizers of this Conference, and establish a two-way exchange of ideas between the academic community of this University and racial and ethnic communities.

We are making a start here and now. Let it be a beginning of a long-lasting and mutually beneficial association between Town and Gown.


TERESA KOTT was born in Poland and educated in Poland, England, and Canada. She holds an M.A. degree in Sociology from the University of Toronto. She has always been involved in public affairs and community work. For ten years she held one of the top offices in the National Executive of the Canadian Polish Congress. Two years ago she was appointed to the Ontario Advisory Council on Multiculturalism. She has her own column in the *Polish Voice Weekly*. Currently, Mrs. Kott teaches a Stong College Tutorial at York on Multiculturalism.

# Unity and Diversity
# in a Transcultural Context

### Hédi Bouraoui

Today we Canadians are confronted by a paradox: the ideal of reconciling two apparently contradictory *idées-forces*: unity, and pluralism. I am not simply adopting and adapting the motto of the United States: "E Pluribus Unum," one out of many. That approach would lead us straight back to Israel Zangwill's image of the "melting pot" which is customarily contrasted to that other cliché, the Canadian "mosaic." I would like to stress, however, that I am at least as concerned with the "many," the "diversity," as the one, the unity. It seems to me that we can strike a balance between the "melting pot" and the "mosaic" by substituting for two misleading, though beguiling, metaphors the notion of Transculturalism.

The linguistic charge sometimes blinds us to the real issues, so I will begin with some basic definitions. I defined the notion of Transculturalism in a theoretical paper last year and will therefore not repeat its argument at length. But briefly speaking, I was dissatisfied with the term "Multiculturalism" which has become banal and misleading. It is too often taken to mean "the Others," as opposed to ourselves, the majority. It is too closely identified with the Canadian mosaic, in which individual groups and traditions are respected, but sometimes at the expense of Canadian identity. The "melting pot" ideal, on the other hand, seems dangerously close to the definition provided cogently, and with no conscious irony, by a first-year Humanities student: "There is this big pot and they put all the new immigrants into it and melt them down." But, as I asked before, what shape do they assume when this amorphous mass oozes from the pot? In other words, both mosaic and melting pot are extremes. In the former, assimilation may be minimal; and in the latter, all traditions may be lost when immigrants are absorbed by the majority group.

Transculturalism represents an attempt to fill the gap between the little pieces of the mosaic until there is no longer a mosaic at all — but neither is there a shapeless blob. It involves integrating different groups in a humanistic way, and arousing their curiosity about each other so as to build bridges between peoples — Italians learning about Ukrainians, and so on.

If this seems a dialectical and philosophic approach, it is important to remember that the currently "hot" topic of the national unity was itself born out of the threat posed by Québec separatism. When Québec threatened to cut the umbilical cord and toddle into the world all by itself, the mother country was suddenly shocked to discover that she could not bear to see the old home broken up. The Parti Québécois concept of "sovereignty association" was designed to soften the blow, retaining economic ties combined with what amounts to "home rule" (to borrow the phrase of the Scottish Nationalists). A referendum also sugar-coats the democratic pill for the rest of the country.

Members of the different cultural groups in Canada and the academic community have been debating the question of unity and diversity for years. But the discussion falls on deaf ears until the economic argument is used, for it is this aspect that strikes fear into Canadians.

Ironically, it is because we have failed to pay attention to culture that economics has now focused attention on the discontent of many of our peoples. I would like to see the debate shift back to the ground of culture. We live in an atmosphere where the media have helped to create fear and artificial polarities. By definition, bad news — racial incidents on the subway, alleged racism on the police force, supposed paranoia among new immigrants — receives more publicity than good news — community self-help projects, day care for children of new Canadian working mothers, English as a Second Language.

Diversity can too often mean a lack of common ground. But it can also be a positive force to take into account in creating a national character. As I have said elsewhere, "La culture, c'est le chemin de la tolérance."[1] Cultural diversity can be the cement holding society together, an integrating factor, but only if we build bridges of understanding.

It is an unfortunate truism that Canadians usually begin with negative attitudes — that is, they define themselves by opposition; by what they are not, rather than by what they are. As I mentioned in my article, "Living Next Door to an Elephant," they are so preoccupied with demonstrating that they are not Americans, that they often lose sight of what it is to be, simply, Canadians.[2]

Not that defining by opposition is unique to Canada. As John Porter pointed out in 1972, both the United States and Canada have asserted the value of "ethnicity" or "multiculturalism" in a defensive response to, in Canada, "the assertion of Quebec nationalism," and, in the United States, "the demands of non-white power groups particularly at the community level."[3] Porter also accuses both Americans and Canadians of using the concepts "ethnicity" and "multiculturalism" to protect the economic status quo. He fears that the majority culture, consciously or unconsciously, tries to maintain a kind of working-class ghetto of people perceived as "ethnic." To this end, it promotes pride in ethnicity as a form of compensation. As Porter writes, "One of the most compelling arguments for the maintenance of strong ethnic affiliations, is to enhance the self-concept of members of low status groups."[4] For this reason he himself comes down ultimately on the side of liberal assimilation.[5]

It seems to me, however, that between ethnicity and total assimilation there is a third alternative, and that is the pursuit of an enlightened, tolerant policy of Transculturalism. Such a policy would affirm the unicity of the Canadian experience. By "unicity" I do not mean either "Anglo-conformity" or "Franco-conformity," but a dialogue between and among peoples which will highlight their common experience as Canadians, as well as the rich heritage their original cultures have left and will leave to the New World.

Some historians have felt that immigrants to Canada and the United States were already Canadians and Americans before they came. That is, the New World has tended to attract a particular kind of human being, one reluctant to accept the static society of a mother country, perhaps; one who is ambitious and highly motivated — who has, above all, *chosen* his adopted country.

The choice of loyalty is a factor that strengthens the fabric of Canadian society. Ironically, the majority culture and the government are often unaware of this source of potential support for their position. New immigrants tend to demonstrate what some consider an excess of blind or unquestioning patriotism. Their attitude is perfectly comprehensible. Those who have come to better their lives economically are grateful that their efforts are rewarded. Many have come for political reasons from authoritarian, even totalitarian, societies. The *relative* freedom of speech in Canada may seem absolute to them compared to the repressive censorship of their homeland. They may turn a blind eye to activities that anger civil libertarians, such as the RCMP opening private mail. At the extreme, some immigrants adopt the attitude that Canada is "my country, right or wrong."

The vast majority of immigrants are overwhelmingly thankful for their lot in Canada. But should not Canada also be grateful to the immigrants? Certainly political refugees and those who have been economically deprived have strong reasons for their appreciation. But both they and members of the Canadian majority culture (or two majority cultures) should be aware that they are paying back their debt many times over. They must work harder to establish themselves, frequently in positions the native-born refuse to consider. They infuse new blood and old skills — technical and professional — into society. The Toronto skyline, for instance, would not be in the world-class it is today were it not for the Italian and German construction workers and skilled tradesmen who arrived in time to contribute to the building boom of the 1960s. What native Torontonian would like to see his or her city move back twenty years in time when many North Americans (including the good people of Montréal) perceived it as the quintessence of provincial boredom: Hogtown, Toronto the Good?

Unity is only a myth to be exploded. No nation is ever "unified" in the sense of being homogeneous. There are always different political parties, or, even within a single-party system, factions. The sole "unity" we must strive for in Canada is universal participation — in political, but above all in cultural processes. Perhaps it is not a monolithic unity we are seeking at all, but rather uniqueness, which stems from cultural diversity.

We began hearing about Multiculturalism in the early 1970s

when it was feared that the emphasis on bilingualism and biculturalism would inevitably lead to an inferiority complex on the part of "the
others." Transculturalism should ideally lead to a sense of "the
otherness of others," an ability to empathize with difference as well as
resemblance. From the newcomer's point of view, it should lead to
dignity and self-respect. Fernan Carrière, writing in *Le Temps*
[Ottawa], thinking primarily of the Franco-Ontarian presence, could
be describing the contributions of all cultures: "L'unité nationale
commence par la fin du mépris et la fin du mépris commence par le
respect de soi."[6]

Canadians of long standing need to put forth antennae sensitive
to the feelings of newcomers. One cannot jealously guard prerogatives
simply because one's ancestors happened to arrive earlier. By that
yardstick, the Indians and Esquimaux would have the greatest rights.
And the lot of the Canadian Indian, while better in most respects than
that of his counterpart south of the border, still leaves a great deal to
be desired. As Leo Driedger points out, the native peoples constitute
69% of the population in the Canadian North, but only a tiny
percentage of our total population. Therefore, although they are
"multilingual and multicultural," their small numbers, and often the
lack of treaties with the government, make them "economically and
politically powerless."[7] After the native peoples, the French Canadians were the first group to settle in large numbers, yet their
situation has remained inferior to that of the Anglo-Saxons who
ultimately took over the country. As Driedger says, the real issue is
that "Although legally of equal status, the French have always been
junior partners in the alliance with the British."[8]

Sometimes newer cultural groups as well can infringe on the
rights of other groups which are less numerous, less well-organized,
or less vocal than themselves. In Toronto itself — the familiar
microcosm of Canadian society — Central European Jews, by number
and by date of arrival, have been a strong force. They can be described
as an "achieving minority" (Ralf Dahrendorf's term). Now the Italian
community is coming into its own. But smaller communities may be
lost in the shuffle — there may not be enough of them to be courted
by politicians for their votes, or by colleges and universities for their
children.

Multiculturalism is too often taken to mean a way of keeping the
lid on recent immigrants, of binding diverse people under the same

political frame. Its debate coincides with the recent rapid influx of new immigrant strains into urban areas of southern Ontario, resulting in culture shocks and fears on both sides.

Transculturalism, on the other hand, takes a longer, more philosophic view. It represents an attempt to ensure that all special interest groups are heard, not only by the majority, but also by each other. In the 1830s Alexis de Tocqueville warned of one potential danger inherent in democracy: that is, the "tyranny of the majority." Canada should be careful that all groups receive equal, fair, balanced attention, to avoid any tyranny of either majority or minority.

There may be strength in numbers, but there is also strength in diversity. De Tocqueville felt that conformity is the concomitant of majority rule. James Baldwin deplores and mocks "the American ideal," "that everyone should be as much alike as possible."[9] Ralf Dahrendorf also complains of "that homogeneity which breeds boredom and kills creativity."

John Stuart Mill's famous essay, "On Liberty," asserts that a society which values conformity is likely to stifle eccentricity. To tolerate eccentricity is to allow genius to flower: "Eccentricity has always abounded when and where strength of character has abounded; and the amount of eccentricity in a society has generally been proportional to the amount of genius, mental vigor, and moral courage it contained."[10]

It seems that most Québécois would likely favor some form of federation with, at the most, sovereignty association rather than separation. The other groups composing Canadian society as well want above all to have "droit au chapitre," the right to be heard. The uprooting of peoples has always been regarded negatively. But the newcomer may offer a fresh critical perspective and new ideas if Canada will listen. It is not conformity which will lead to unity (or unicity), but rather diversity defined as a positive, as the force that can shape the national character.

If we grant everyone the right to be different, we will benefit from cultural enrichment and construct a unique, creative, tolerant Canadian identity. As the Minister of State for Multiculturalism, the Hon. Steve Paproski, said, the "Community of Communities" (the Prime Minister's phrase for Canada) "is a treasured resource that must be celebrated and not merely tolerated or feared."[11] Canada is already a pluralistic society, but we must work at changing values in a humanistic way if we are to profit from that fact. Political accessibility is not enough; to assure it remains the province of a relatively small government ministry. Political change is merely the structure; a change in attitudes involves the total culture and every individual in it. We are taking some of the first steps this weekend towards a Transcultural participation that will indeed be cause for celebration. We hope in the near future to continue our progress away from a merely hypothetical unity growing out of a fear of separatism, towards a uniqueness in which we not only live with our differences, but rejoice in them.

## Notes

1   "Rencontre avec Hédi Bouraoui," Propos recueillis par Rafik Ben Zina, *L'Action*, 1 aout. 1979, pp. 6-7.
2   "Living Next Door to an Elephant: Canadian Reactions to the American Ethos," *Life Styles: Diversity in American Society*, ed. Saul D. Feldman and Gerald W. Thielbar, 2nd ed. (Boston: Little, Brown, 1975), pp. 45-58.
3   John Porter, "Dilemmas and Contradictions of a Multi-Ethnic Society," Paper Delivered to Royal Society of Canada, St. John's, Newfoundland, June 1972, p 6.
4   Porter, p. 12.
5   Porter, p. 17.
6   "Pour un tourisme engagé . . .": Chronique de voyage, *Le Temps*, 1, No. 8 (sept. 1979), 1.
7   Leo Driedger, "Identity in the Canadian Mosaic," *The Canadian Ethnic Mosaic: A Quest for Identity* (Toronto: McClelland and Stewart, 1978), p. 10.
8   Driedger, p. 13.
9   James Baldwin, "The Harlem Ghetto," *Notes of a Native Son* (Boston: Beacon, 1955), p. 65.
10  York University Address, Oct. 1979, p. 6.
11  "Notes for an Address by the Hon. Steve Paproski, Minister of State, Multiculturalism," to the Biennial Conference of the Canadian Ethnic Studies Association, Vancouver, 13 Oct. 1979.